D1242023

AN ESSAY ON THE NATURE AND
SIGNIFICANCE OF ECONOMIC SCIENCE

MACMILLAN AND CO., Limited
LONDON · BOMBAY · CALCUTTA · MADRAS
MELBOURNE

THE MACMILLAN COMPANY
NEW YORK · BOSTON · CHICAGO
DALLAS · ATLANTA · SAN FRANCISCO

THE MACMILLAN COMPANY
OF CANADA, LIMITED
TORONTO

The Mises Institute
Auburn, Alabama
2007

AN ESSAY ON THE
NATURE & SIGNIFICANCE
OF ECONOMIC SCIENCE

BY

LIONEL ROBBINS

Professor of Economics in the University of London

MACMILLAN & CO., LIMITED
ST. MARTIN'S STREET, LONDON
1932

Mises Institute
Auburn, Alabama
2007

TO MY FATHER

PREFACE

THE purpose of this Essay is twofold. In the first place, it seeks to arrive at precise notions concerning the subject-matter of Economic Science and the nature of the generalisations of which Economic Science consists. Secondly it attempts to explain the limitations and the significance of these generalisations, both as a guide to the interpretation of reality and as a basis for political practice. At the present day, as a result of the theoretical developments of the last sixty years, there is no longer any ground for serious differences of opinion on these matters, once the issues are clearly stated. Yet, for lack of such statement, confusion still persists in many quarters, and false ideas are prevalent with regard to the pre-occupations of the economist and the nature and the extent of his competence. As a result, the reputation of Economics suffers, and full advantage is not taken of the knowledge it confers. This Essay is an attempt to remedy this deficiency—to make clear what it is that economists discuss and what may legitimately be expected as a result of their discussions. Thus on the one hand it may be regarded as a commentary on the methods and assumptions of pure theory: on the other hand, as a series of prolegomena to work in Applied Economics.

The object of the Essay necessitates the taking of broad views. But my aim throughout has been to keep as close to earth as possible. I have eschewed philosophical refinements as falling outside the province in which I have any claim to professional competence; and I have based my propositions on the actual practice of the best modern works on the subject. In a study of this sort, written by an economist for fellow-economists, it seemed better to try to drive home the argument by continual reference to accepted solutions of particular problems, than to elaborate, out of the void, a theory of what Economics should become. At the same time, I have tried to be brief. My object has been to suggest a point of view rather than to treat the subject in all its details. To do this it seemed desirable to be concise even at the expense of sacrificing much material which I had originally collected. I hope, however, at a later stage to publish a work on general Economic Theory in which the principles here laid down are further illustrated and amplified.

For the views which I have advanced, I make no claim whatever to originality. I venture to hope that in one or two instances I have succeeded in giving expository force to certain principles not always clearly stated. But, in the main, my object has been to state, as simply as I could, propositions which are the common property of most modern economists. I owe much to conversations with my colleagues and pupils at the School of Economics. For the rest I have acknowledged in footnotes the debts of which I am chiefly conscious. I should like, however, once more to acknowledge my especial indebtedness to the works of Professor Ludwig von Mises and to the *Commonsense of Political Economy* of the late Philip Wicksteed. The considerable extent to which I have cited these sources is yet a very inadequate reflection of the general assistance which I have derived from their use.

LIONEL ROBBINS.

THE LONDON SCHOOL OF ECONOMICS,
February, 1932.

CONTENTS

CHAPTER I

CHAPTER II

CHAPTER III

CHAPTER IV

CHAPTER V

CHAPTER VI

CHAPTER I

THE SUBJECT-MATTER OF ECONOMICS

1. The object of this Essay is to exhibit the nature and significance of Economic Science. Its first task therefore is to delimit the subject-matter of Economics —to provide a working definition of what Economics is about.

Unfortunately, this is by no means as simple as it sounds. The efforts of economists during the last hundred and fifty years have resulted in the establishment of a body of generalisations whose substantial accuracy and importance are open to question only by the ignorant or the perverse. But they have achieved no unanimity concerning the ultimate nature of the common subject-matter of these generalisations. The central chapters of the standard works on Economics retail, with only minor variations, the main principles of the Science. But the chapters in which the object of the work is explained still present wide divergences. We all talk about the same things, but we have not yet agreed what it is we are talking about.[1]

[1] Lest this should be thought an overstatement I subjoin below a few characteristic definitions. I have confined my choice to Anglo-Saxon literature because, as will be shown later on, a more satisfactory state of affairs is coming to prevail elsewhere. "Economics is a study of men earning a living" (Marshall, *Principles*, p. 1). "Economics is the science which treats phenomena from the standpoint of price" (Davenport, *Economics*

1

This is not in any way an unexpected or a disgraceful circumstance. As Mill pointed out a hundred years ago, the definition of a science has almost invariably, not preceded, but followed the creation of the science itself. "Like the wall of a city it has usually been erected, not to be a receptacle for such edifices as might afterwards spring up, but to circumscribe an aggregate already in existence."[1] Indeed, it follows from the very nature of a science that until it has reached a certain stage of development, definition of its scope is necessarily impossible. For the unity of a science only shows itself in the unity of the problems it is able to solve, and such unity is not discovered until the interconnection of its explanatory principles has been established.[2] Modern Economics takes its rise from various separate spheres of practical and philosophical enquiry—from investigations of the Balance of Trade—from discussions of the legitimacy of the taking of interest.[3] It was not until quite recent times that it had become sufficiently unified for the

---

of Enterprise, p. 25). "The aim of Political Economy is the explanation of the general causes on which the material welfare of human beings depends" (Cannan, *Elementary Political Economy*, p. 1). "It is too wide a definition to speak of Economics as the science of the material side of human welfare." Economics is "the study of the general methods by which men co-operate to meet their material needs" (Beveridge, *Economics as a Liberal Education, Economica*, vol. i., p. 3). Economics, according to Professor Pigou, is the study of economic welfare, economic welfare being defined as "that part of welfare which can be brought directly or indirectly into relation with the measuring rod of money" (*Economics of Welfare*, 3rd edition, p. 1). The sequel will show how widely the implications of these definitions diverge from one another.

[1] *Unsettled Questions of Political Economy*, p. 120.

[2] "Nicht die '*sachlichen*' Zusammenhänge der 'Dinge' sondern die *gedanklichen* Zusammenhänge der *Probleme* legen den Arbeitsgebieten der Wissenschaften zugrunde" (Max Weber, *Die Objectivität Sozialwissenschaftlichen und Sozialpolitischen Erkenntnis, Gesammelte Aufsätze zur Wissenschaftslehre*, p. 166).

[3] See Cannan, *Review of Economic Theory*, pp. 1-35, and Schumpeter, *Epochen der Methoden- und Dogmengeschichte*, pp. 21-38.

identity of the problems underlying these different enquiries to be detected. At an earlier stage, any attempt to discover the ultimate nature of the science was necessarily doomed to disaster. It would have been waste of time to have attempted it.

But once this stage of unification has been reached not only is it not waste of time to attempt precise delimitation; it is waste of time not to do so. Further elaboration can only take place if the objective is clearly indicated. The problems are no longer suggested by naïve reflection. They are indicated by gaps in the unity of theory, by insufficiencies in its explanatory principles. Unless one has grasped what this unity is, one is apt to go off on false scents. There can be little doubt that one of the greatest dangers which beset the modern economist is preoccupation with the irrelevant—the multiplication of activities having little or no connection with the solution of problems strictly germane to his subject.[1] There can be equally little doubt that, in those centres where questions of this sort are on the way to ultimate settlement, the solution of the central theoretical problems proceeds most rapidly. Moreover, if these solutions are to be fruitfully applied, if we are to understand correctly the bearing of Economic Science on practice, it is essential that we should know exactly the implications and limitations of the generalisations it establishes. It is therefore with an easy conscience that we may advance to what, at first sight, is the extremely academic problem of finding a formula to describe the general subject-matter of Economics.

[1] See Chapter II., Section 4, especially the footnote on p. 40, for further elaboration of this point.

2. The definition of Economics which would probably command most adherents, at any rate in Anglo-
Saxon countries, is that which relates it to the study
of the causes of material welfare. This element is
common to the definitions of Cannan[1] and Marshall,[2]
and even Pareto, whose approach[3] in so many ways
was so different from that of the two English economists, gives it the sanction of his usage. It is implied,
too, in the definition of J. B. Clark.[4]

And, at first sight, it must be admitted, it certainly
does appear as if we have here a definition which for
practical purposes describes the object of our interest.
In ordinary speech there is unquestionably a sense in
which the word "economic" is used as equivalent to
"material". One has only to reflect upon its signi-
fication to the layman in such phrases as "Economic
History",[5] or "a conflict between economic and
political advantage", to realise the extreme plausibility of this interpretation. No doubt there are some
matters falling outside this definition which seem to
fall within the scope of Economics, but these may
very well seem to be of the order of marginal cases
inevitable with every definition.

But the final test of the validity of any such definition is not its apparent harmony with certain usages
of everyday speech, but its capacity to describe
exactly the ultimate subject-matter of the main

---

[1] *Wealth*, 1st edition, p. 17.
[2] *Principles*, 8th edition, p. 1.
[3] *Cours d'Economie Politique*, p. 6.
[4] *Essentials of Economic Theory*, p. 5. See also *Philosophy of Wealth*,
ch. i. In this chapter the difficulties discussed below are explicitly recognised, but, surprisingly enough, instead of this leading to a rejection of the
definition, it leads only to a most perverse attempt to change the significance
of the word "material".
[5] But see Chapter II. below for an examination of the validity of this
interpretation.

generalisations of the science.[1] And when we submit
the definition in question to this test, it is seen to
possess deficiencies which, so far from being marginal
and subsidiary, amount to nothing less than a complete failure to exhibit either the scope or the significance of the most central generalisations of all.

Let us take any one of the main divisions of theoretical Economics and examine to what extent it is covered
by the definition we are examining. We should all
agree, for instance, that a Theory of Wages was an
integral part of any system of economic analysis. Can
we be content with the assumption that the phenomena
with which such a theory has to deal are adequately
described as pertaining to the more material side of
human welfare?

Wages, in the strict sense of the term, are sums
earned by the performance of work at stipulated rates
under the supervision of an employer. In the looser
sense in which the term is often used in general
economic analysis, it stands for labour incomes other
than profits. Now it is perfectly true that some wages
are the price of work which may be described as conducive to material welfare—the wages of a sewage
collector, for instance. But it is equally true that some

[1] In this connection it is perhaps worth while clearing up a confusion
which not infrequently occurs in discussions of terminology. It is often
urged that scientific definitions of words used both in ordinary language
and in scientific analysis should not depart from the usages of everyday
speech. No doubt this is a counsel of perfection, but in principle the main
contention may be accepted. Appalling confusion is created when a word
which is used in one sense in business practice is used in another sense in
the analysis of such practice. One has only to think of the difficulties which
have been created by such departures in regard to the meaning of the term
capital. But it is one thing to follow everyday usage when appropriating
a term. It is another thing to contend that everyday speech is the final
court of appeal when defining a science. For in this case the significant
implication of the word *is* the subject-matter of the generalisations of the
science. And it is only by reference to these that the definition can finally
be established. Any other procedure would be intolerable.

wages, the wages of the members of an orchestra, for instance, are paid for work which has not the remotest bearing on material welfare. Yet the one set of services, equally with the other, commands a price and enters into the circle of exchange. The Theory of Wages is as applicable to the explanation of the latter as it is to the explanation of the former. Its elucidations are not limited to wages which are paid for work ministering to the "more material" side of human well-being—whatever that may be.

Nor is the situation saved if we turn from the work for which wages are paid to the things on which wages are spent. It might be urged that it is not because what the wage-earner produces is conducive to other people's material welfare that the Theory of Wages may be subsumed under the description, but because what he gets is conducive to his own. But this does not bear examination for an instant. The wage-earner may buy bread with his earnings. But he may buy a seat at the theatre. A theory of wages which ignored all those sums which were paid for "immaterial" services or spent on "immaterial" ends would be intolerable. The circle of exchange would be hopelessly ruptured. The whole process of static analysis could never be employed. It is impossible to conceive significant generalisations about a field thus arbitrarily delimited.

It is improbable that any serious economist has attempted to delimit Wage Theory in this manner, however much he may have attempted thus to delimit the whole body of generalisations of which Wage Theory is a part. But attempts have certainly been made to deny the applicability of economic analysis to the examination of the achievement of

ends other than material welfare. No less an economist than Professor Cannan has urged that the
Political Economy of War is "a contradiction in
terms",[1] apparently on the ground that, since Economics is concerned with the causes of material welfare,
and since war is not a cause of material welfare, war
cannot be part of the subject-matter of Economics.
As a moral judgment on the uses to which abstract
knowledge should be put, Professor Cannan's strictures
may be accepted. But it is abundantly clear, as
Professor Cannan's own practice has shown, that, so
far from Economics having no light to throw on the
successful prosecution of modern warfare, it is highly
doubtful whether the organisers of war can possibly
do without it. It is a curious paradox that Professor
Cannan's pronouncement on this matter should occur
in a work which, more than any other published in
our language, uses the apparatus of economic analysis
to illuminate many of the most urgent and the most
intricate problems of a community organised for war.

This habit on the part of modern English economists
of describing Economics as concerned with the causes
of material welfare, is all the more curious when we
reflect upon the unanimity with which they have
adopted a non-material definition of "productivity".
Adam Smith, it will be remembered, distinguished
between Productive and Unproductive Labour,
according as the efforts in question did or did
not result in the production of a tangible material
object. "The labour of some of the most respectable
orders in the society is, like that of menial servants,
unproductive of any value and does not fix or realise
itself in any permanent subject or vendible commodity

1 Cannan, *An Economist's Protest*, p. 49.

which endures after that labour is past. . . . The sovereign, for example, with all the officers both of justice and war who serve under him are unproductive labourers. . . . In the same class must be ranked some both of the gravest and most important, and some of the most frivolous professions: churchmen, lawyers, physicians, men of letters of all kinds; players, buffoons, musicians, opera singers, opera dancers, etc. . . ."[1] Modern economists, Professor Cannan foremost among them,[2] have rejected this conception of productivity as inadequate.[3] So long as it is the object of demand, whether privately or collectively formulated, the labour of the opera singers and dancers must be regarded as "productive". But productive of what? Of material welfare because it cheers the business man and releases new stores of energy to organise the production of material? That way lies dilettantism and *Wortspielerei*. It is productive because it is valued, because it has specific importance for various "economic subjects". So far is modern theory from the point of view of Adam Smith and the Physiocrats that the epithet of productive labour is denied even to the production of material objects, if the material objects are not valuable. Indeed, it has gone further than this. Professor Fisher, among others, has demonstrated conclusively[4] that the income from a material object must in the last resort be conceived as an "immaterial"

---

[1] *Wealth of Nations* (Cannan's ed.), p. 315.

[2] *Theories of Production and Distribution*, pp. 18-31; *Review of Economic Theory*, pp. 49-51.

[3] It is even arguable that the reaction has gone too far. Whatever its demerits, the Smithian classification had a significance for capital theory which in recent times has not always been clearly recognised. See Taussig, *Wages and Capital*, pp. 132-151.

[4] *The Nature of Capital and Income*, ch. vii.

use. From my house equally as from my valet or the services of the opera singer, I derive an income which "perishes in the moment of its production".

But, if this is so, is it not misleading to go on describing Economics as the study of the causes of material welfare? The services of the opera dancer are wealth. Economics deals with the pricing of these services, equally with the pricing of the services of a cook. Whatever Economics is concerned with, it is *not* concerned with the causes of material welfare as such.

The causes which have led to the persistence of this definition are mainly historical in character. It is the last vestige of Physiocratic influence. English economists are not usually interested in questions of scope and method. In nine cases out of ten where this definition occurs, it has probably been taken over quite uncritically from some earlier work. But, in the case of Professor Cannan, its retention is due to more positive causes; and it is instructive to attempt to trace the processes of reasoning which seem to have rendered it plausible to so penetrating and so acute an intellect.

The rationale of any definition is usually to be found in the use which is actually made of it. Professor Cannan develops his definition in close juxtaposition to a discussion of "the Fundamental Conditions of Wealth for Isolated Man and for Society",[1] and it is in connection with this discussion that he actually uses his conception of what is economic and what is not. It is no accident, it may be suggested, that if the approach to economic analysis is made from this point of view, the "materialist" definition, as we may

[1] This is the title of ch. ii. of *Wealth* (1st edition).

call it, has the maximum plausibility. This deserves vindication in some detail.

Professor Cannan commences by contemplating the activities of a man isolated completely from society and enquiring what conditions will determine his wealth—that is to say, his material welfare. In such conditions, a division of activities into "economic" and "non-economic"—activities directed to the increase of material welfare and activities directed to the increase of non-material welfare —has a certain plausibility. If Robinson Crusoe digs potatoes, he is pursuing material or "economic" welfare. If he talks to the parrot, his activities are "non-economic" in character. There is a difficulty here to which we must return later, but it is clear *prima facie* that, in this context, the distinction is not ridiculous.

But let us suppose Crusoe is rescued and, coming home, goes on the stage and talks to the parrot for a living. Surely in such conditions these conversations have an economic aspect. Whether he spends his earnings on potatoes or philosophy, Crusoe's getting and spending are capable of being exhibited in terms of the fundamental economic categories.

Professor Cannan does not pause to ask whether his distinction is very helpful in the analysis of an exchange economy—though, after all, it is here that economic generalisations have the greatest practical utility. Instead, he proceeds forthwith to consider the "fundamental conditions of wealth" for society considered as a whole. And here again his definition becomes plausible: once more the aggregate of social activities can be sorted out into the twofold classification it implies. Some activities are devoted to the pursuit of material welfare: some are not. We think, for instance, of the executive of a communist society, deciding to spend so much labour-time on the provision of bread, so much on the provision of circuses.

But even here and in the earlier case of the Crusoe Economy, the procedure is open to what is surely a crushing objection. Let us accept Professor Cannan's use of the terms "economic" and "non-economic" as being equivalent to conducive to material and non-material welfare respectively. Then we may say with him that the wealth of society will be greater the greater proportion of time which is devoted to material ends, the less the proportion which is devoted to immaterial ends. We may say this. But we must also admit that, using the word "economic" in a perfectly normal sense, there still remains an economic problem, both for society and for the individual, of choosing between these two kinds of activity—a problem of how, given the relative valuations of product and leisure and the opportunities of production, the fixed supply of twenty-four hours in the day is to be divided between them. *There is still an economic problem of deciding between the "economic" and the "non-economic".* One of the main problems of the Theory of Production lies half outside Professor Cannan's definition.

Is not this in itself a sufficient argument for its abandonment?[1]

---

[1] There are other quarrels which we might pick with this particular definition. As Dr. Benham has pointed out (*The Concept of Economic Welfare* [*Economica*, June, 1930]), the whole concept of welfare is suspect as the subject-matter of a scientific study. From the philosophical point of view, the term "material welfare" is a very odd construction. "The material causes of welfare" might be admitted. But "material welfare" seems to involve a division of states of mind which are essentially unitary. For the purposes of this chapter, however, it has seemed better to ignore these deficiencies and to concentrate on the main question, namely, whether the definition can in any way describe the contents of which it is intended to serve as a label.

3. But where, then, are we to turn? The position is by no means hopeless. Our critical examination of the "materialist" definition has brought us to a point from which it is possible to proceed forthwith to formulate a definition which shall be immune from all these strictures.

Let us turn back to the simplest case in which we found Professor Cannan's terminology inappropriate—the case of isolated man dividing his time between the production of real income and the enjoyment of leisure. We have just seen that such a division may legitimately be said to have an economic aspect. Wherein does this aspect consist?

The answer is to be found in the formulation of the exact conditions which make such division necessary. They are three. In the first place, isolated man wants both real income and leisure. Secondly, he has not enough of either fully to satisfy his want of each. Thirdly, he can spend his time in augmenting his real income or he can spend it in taking more leisure. Therefore he has to choose. He has to economise. Whether he chooses with deliberation or not, his behaviour has the form of choice. The disposition of his time and his resources has a relationship to his system of wants. It has an economic aspect.

This example is typical of the whole field of Economic Studies. From the point of view of the economist, the conditions of human existence exhibit three fundamental characteristics. The ends[1] are various. The time and the means for achieving

---

[1] On the sense in which "end" is to be understood to be formulated, there are further elucidations in the next chapter. From our point of view here it is simply to be taken as an objective of conduct. No indeterministic view of behaviour is intended to be implied.

these ends are at once limited and capable of alternative application. Here we are, sentient creatures with bundles of desires and aspirations, with masses of instinctive tendencies all urging us in different ways to action. But the time in which these tendencies can be expressed is limited. The external world does not offer full opportunities for their complete achievement. Life is short. Nature is niggardly. Our fellows have other objectives. Yet we can use our lives for doing different things, our materials and the services of others for achieving different objectives.

Now *by itself* the multiplicity of ends has no necessary interest for the economist. If I want to do two things, and I have ample time and ample means with which to do them, and I do not want the time or the means for anything else, then my conduct assumes none of those forms which are the subject of economic science. Nirvana is not necessarily single bliss. It is merely the complete satisfaction of *all* requirements.

Nor is the mere limitation of means *by itself* sufficient to give rise to economic phenomena. If means of satisfaction have no alternative use, then they may be scarce, but they cannot be economised. The Manna which fell from heaven may have been scarce, but, if it was impossible to exchange it for something else or to postpone its use, it was not the subject of any activity with an economic aspect.

But when time and the means for achieving ends are limited *and* capable of alternative application, then behaviour necessarily assumes the form of choice. Every act which involves time and scarce means for the achievement of one end involves the relinquishment of their use for the achievement of another. It has an economic aspect.[1] If I want bread and sleep, and in the time at my disposal I cannot have all I want of both, then some part of my wants of bread and sleep must go unsatisfied. If, in a limited lifetime, I would wish to be both a philosopher and a mathematician, but my rate of acquisition of knowledge is such that I cannot do both completely, then some part of my wish for philosophical or mathematical competence or both must be relinquished.

Now not all the means for achieving human ends are limited. There are things in the external world which are present in such comparative abundance that the use of particular units for one thing does not involve going without other units for others. The air which we breathe, for instance, is such a "free" commodity. Save in very special circumstances, the fact that we need air imposes no sacrifice of time or resources. The loss of one cubic foot of air implies no sacrifice of alternatives. Units of air have no specific significance for conduct. And it is conceivable that living creatures may exist whose "ends" are so limited that all goods for them are "free" goods, that no goods have specific significance.

But, in general, human activity with its multiplicity of objectives has not this independence of time or specific resources. The time at our disposal is limited. There are only twenty-four hours in the day. We have to choose between the different uses to which they may be put.[2] The services which others put at our disposal are limited. The material

[1] Cp. Schönfield, *Grenznutzen und Wirtschaftsrechnung*, p. 1; Hans Mayer, *Untersuchungen zu dem Grundgesetze der Wirtschaftlichen Wertrechnung* (*Zeitschrift für Volkswirtschaft und Sozialpolitik*, Bd. 2, p. 123).

[2] See Mises, *Die Gemeinwirtschaft*, p. 98; also *Soziologie und Geschichte* (*Archiv für Sozialwissenschaft und Sozialpolitik*, Bd. 61, Heft 3, especially pp. 471-484).

means of achieving ends are limited. We have been turned out of Paradise. We have neither eternal life nor unlimited means of gratification. Everywhere we turn, if we choose one thing we must relinquish others which, in different circumstances, we would wish not to have relinquished. Scarcity of means to satisfy given ends is an almost ubiquitous condition of human behaviour.

Here, then, is the unity of subject of Economic Science, the forms assumed by human behaviour in disposing of scarce means. The examples we have discussed already harmonise perfectly with this conception. Both the services of cooks and the services of opera dancers are limited in relation to demand and can be put to alternative uses. The Theory of Wages in its entirety is covered by our present definition. So, too, is the Political Economy of War. The waging of war necessarily involves the withdrawal of scarce goods and services from other uses if it is to be satisfactorily achieved. It has therefore an economic aspect. The economist studies the disposal of scarce means. He is interested in the way different degrees of scarcity of different goods give rise to different ratios of valuation between them, and he is interested in the way in which changes in conditions of scarcity, whether coming from changes in ends or changes in means—from the demand side or the supply side—affect these ratios. Economics is the science which studies human behaviour as a relationship between ends and scarce means which have alternative uses.[1]

[1] Cp. Menger, *Grundsätze der Volkswirtschaftslehre*, 1te aufl., pp. 51-70; Mises, *Die Gemeinwirtschaft*, pp. 98 *seq.*; Fetter, *Economic Principles*, ch. i.; Strigl, *Die Ökonomischen Katagorien und die Organisation der Wirtschaft*, *passim*; Mayer, *op. cit.*

4. It is important at once to notice certain implications of this conception. The conception we have rejected, the conception of Economics as the study of the causes of material welfare, was what may be called a *classificatory* conception. It marks off certain kinds of human behaviour, behaviour directed to the procuring of material welfare, and designates these as the subject-matter of Economics. Other kinds of conduct lie outside the scope of its investigations. The conception we have adopted may be described as *analytical*. It does not attempt to pick out certain *kinds* of behaviour, but focuses attention on a particular *aspect* of behaviour, the form imposed by the influence of scarcity.[1] It follows from this, therefore, that in so far as it offers this aspect, any kind of human behaviour falls within the scope of Economic Generalisations. We do not say that the production of potatoes is economic activity and the production of philosophy is not. We say rather that, in so far as either kind of activity involves the relinquishment of other desired alternatives, it has its economic aspect. There are no limitations on the subject-matter of Economic Science save this.

Certain writers, however, while rejecting the conception of Economics as concerned with material welfare, have sought to impose on its scope a restriction of another nature: They have urged that the behaviour with which Economics is concerned is essentially a certain type of social behaviour, the

[1] On the distinction between analytical and classificatory definitions, see Irving Fisher, *Senses of Capital* (*Economic Journal*, vol. vii., p. 213). It is interesting to observe that the change in the conception of Economics implied by our definition is similar to the change in the conception of capital implied in Professor Fisher's definition. Adam Smith defined capital as a kind of wealth. Professor Fisher would have us regard it as an aspect of wealth.

behaviour implied by the institutions of the In-
dividualist Exchange Economy. On this view, that
kind of behaviour which is not specifically social in
this definite sense is not the subject-matter of Economics. Professor Amonn in particular has devoted
almost infinite pains to elaborating this conception.[1]

Now it may be freely admitted that, within the
wide field of our definition, the attention of economists
is focussed chiefly on the complications of the Exchange
Economy. The reason for this is one of interest. The
activities of isolated man, equally with the activities
of the exchange economy, are subject to the limitations
we are contemplating. But, from the point of view of
isolated man, economic analysis is unnecessary. The
elements of the problem are given to unaided reflection. Examination of the behaviour of a Crusoe may
be immensely illuminating as an aid to more advanced
studies. But, from the point of view of Crusoe, it is
obviously *extra-marginal.* So too in the case of a
"closed" communistic society. Again, from the point
of view of the economist, the comparison of the
phenomena of such a society with those of the ex·
change economy may be very illuminating. But from
the point of view of the members of the executive,
the generalisations of Economics would be un-
interesting. Their position would be analogous to
Crusoe's. For them the economic problem would
be merely whether to apply productive power to
this or to that. Now, as Professor Mises has shown,
given central ownership and control of the means of

---

[1] See his *Objekt und Grundbegriffe der theoretischen Nationalökonomie.*
The criticisms of Schumpeter and Strigl on pp. 110-125 and pp. 155-156 are
particularly important from this point of view. With the very greatest
respect for Professor Amonn's exhaustive analysis, I cannot resist the
impression that he is inclined rather to magnify the degree of his divergence
from the attitude of these two authors.

production, the registering of individual pulls and
resistances by a mechanism of prices and costs is
excluded by definition. It follows therefore that
the decisions of the executive must necessarily be
"arbitrary".[1] That is to say, they must be based on
its valuations—not on the valuations of consumers
and producers. This at once simplifies the form of
choice. Without the guidance of a price system, the
organisation of production must depend on the valuations of the final organiser, just as the organisation
of a patriarchal estate unconnected with a money
economy must depend on the valuations of the
patriarch.

But in the exchange economy the position is much
more complicated. The implications of individual
decisions reach beyond the repercussions on the individual. One may realise completely the implications
for oneself of a decision to spend money in this way
rather than in that way. But it is not so easy to trace
the effects of this decision on the whole complex
of "scarcity relationships"—on wages, on profits, on
prices, on rates of capitalisation, and the organisation
of production. On the contrary, the utmost effort of
abstract thought is required to devise generalisations
which enable us to grasp them. For this reason
economic analysis has most utility in the exchange
economy. It is unnecessary in the isolated economy.
It is debarred from any but the simplest generalisations by the very *raison d'être* of a communist society.
But where independent initiative in social relation-

---

[1] See Mises, *Die Gemeinwirtschaft*, pp. 94-138. In his *Die Lehren des
Marxismus im Lichte der russischen Revolution* and *Planwirtschaft und
Marktwirtschaft in der Sowjet Union* (*Der deutsche Volkswirt Jahrg.*, 1931,
No. 32, pp. 1073-1074), Professor Boris Brutzkus has well shown the way
in which this difficulty has been exemplified in the various phases of the
Russian experiment.

ships is permitted to the individual, there economic analysis comes into its own.

But it is one thing to contend that economic analysis has *most interest and utility* in an exchange economy. It is another to contend that its subject-matter is *limited* to such phenomena. The unjustifiability of this latter contention may be shown conclusively by two considerations. In the first place, it is clear that behaviour outside the exchange economy is conditioned by the same limitation of means in relation to ends as behaviour within the economy, and is capable of being subsumed under the same fundamental categories.[1] The generalisations of the Theory of Value are as applicable to the behaviour of isolated man or the executive authority of a communist society, as to the behaviour of man in an exchange economy— even if they are not so illuminating in such contexts. The exchange relationship is a *technical* incident, a technical incident indeed which gives rise to nearly all the interesting complications, but still, for all that, subsidiary to the main fact of scarcity.

In the second place, it is clear that the phenomena of the exchange economy itself can only be explained by *going behind* such relationships and invoking the operation of those laws of choice which are best seen when contemplating the behaviour of the isolated individual.[2] Professor Amonn seems willing to admit

[1] See Strigl, *op. cit.*, pp. 23-28.
[2] Professor Cassel's dismissal of Crusoe Economics (*Fundamental Thoughts*, p. 27) seems singularly unfortunate since, while the construction of the collectivist state which he favours, is intended to perform exactly the same function, in fact, it suggests possibilities of economic calculation which would not be available to the executive of such a society. Where there is no market for producers' goods, there can be no cost computations based on individual valuations. It is a mistake to suppose that the mere pricing of consumers' goods affords a basis for economic calculation. (See Halm, *Die Konkurrenz*, pp. 34-63.) Moreover, it is only when contemplating the conditions of isolated man that the importance of the alternative

that such a system of pure Economics may be useful as an auxiliary to Economic Science, but he precludes himself from making it the basis of the main system by postulating that the subject-matter of Economics must be defined in terms of the problems discussed by Ricardo. The view that a definition must describe an existing body of knowledge and not lay down arbitrary limits is admirable. But, it may legitimately be asked, why stop at Ricardo?[1] Is it not clear that the imperfections of the Ricardian system were due to just this circumstance that it stopped at the valuations of the market and did not press through to the valuations of the individual? Surely it is the great achievement of the modern Theory of Value to have surmounted just this barrier?[2]

---

applicability of scarce means, which was emphasised above, leaps clearly to the eye. In a social economy of any kind, the mere multiplicity of economic subjects leads one to overlook the possibility of the existence of scarce goods with no alternative uses.

[1] *Op. cit.*, p. 397. On pp. 119-120 Professor Amonn seems to go a long way towards admitting the point made above that the question under dispute relates to the interest, rather than to the limit, of the subject-matter. " Die Nationalökonomie *interessiert* (my italics) am Kaufe nicht die Bedeutung die das einzelne kaufende oder verkaufende Individuum unter seiner individualistisch praktischen Gesichtpunkte diesen Wirtschaftsubjekt beilegt. . . . Erst durch die Setzung einer bestimmten *sozialen* Bedingtheit und unter *dem Gesichtspunkte diesen sozialen Bedingtheit* erlangt die Güterquantitätenveränderung *jene so besonder Kompliziertheit deren Analyse Aufgabe der theoretischen Nationalökonomie ist.*"

[2] The objections outlined above to the definition suggested by Professor Amonn should be sufficient to indicate the nature of the objections to those definitions which run in terms of phenomena from the standpoint of price (Davenport), susceptibility to the "measuring rod of money" (Pigou), or the "science of exchange" (Landry, etc.). Professor Schumpeter, in his *Wesen und Hauptinhalt der theoretischen Nationalökonomie*, has attempted with never to be forgotten subtlety to vindicate the latter definition by demonstrating that it is possible to *conceive* all the fundamental aspects of behaviour germane to Economic Science as having the form of exchange . That this is correct and that it embodies a truth fundamental to the proper understanding of equilibrium theory may be readily admitted. But it is one thing to generalise the notion of exchange as a *construction*. It is another to use it in this sense as a *criterion*. That it *can* function in this way is not disputed. But that it throws the maximum light on the ultimate nature of our subject-matter is surely open to question.

5. Finally, we may return to the definition we rejected and examine how it compares with the definition we have now chosen.

At first sight, it is possible to underestimate the divergence between the two definitions. The one regards the subject-matter of economics as human behaviour conceived as a relationship between ends and means, the other as the causes of material welfare. Scarcity of means and the causes of material welfare—are these not more or less the same thing?

Such a contention rests upon a very crude misconception. It is true that the scarcity of materials is one of the limitations of conduct. But the scarcity of our own time and the services of others is just as important. The scarcity of the services of the schoolmaster and the sewage man have each their economic aspect. Only by saying that services are material vibrations or the like can one stretch the definition to cover the whole field. But this is not only perverse, it is also misleading. In this form the definition may *cover* the field, but it does not describe it. For it is not the *materiality* of even material means of gratification which gives them their status as economic goods; it is their relation to valuations. It is their form rather than their substance which is significant. The "Materialist" conception of economics therefore misrepresents the science as we know it. But the *practice* of those who have adopted it fits in perfectly with our definition. There is no important generalisation in the whole range of Professor Cannan's system which is incompatible with the definition we have chosen.

Moreover, the very example which Professor Cannan selects to illustrate his definition fits much better into our framework than it does into his. "Economists", he says, "would agree that 'Did Bacon write Shakespeare?' was not an economic question, and that the satisfaction which believers in the cryptogram would feel if it were universally accepted would not be an economic satisfaction. . . . On the other hand, they would agree that the controversy would have an economic side if copyright were perpetual and the descendants of Bacon and Shakespeare were disputing the ownership of the plays."[1] Exactly. But why? Because the ownership of the copyright involves material welfare? But the proceeds may all go to missionary societies. Surely the question has an economic aspect simply and solely because the copyright laws supposed would make the use of the plays scarce in relation to the demand for their use, and would in turn provide their owners with command over scarce means of gratification which otherwise would be differently distributed.

[1] *Wealth* (1st edition), ch. i.

CHAPTER II

1. WE have now established a working definition of the subject-matter of Economics. The next step is to examine its implications. In this chapter we shall be concerned with the status of ends and means as they figure in Economic Theory and Economic History. In the next we shall be concerned with the interpretation of various economic "quantities".

2. Let us turn first to the status of ends.[1]

Economics, we have seen, is concerned with that aspect of behaviour which arises from the scarcity of means to achieve given ends. It follows that Economics is entirely neutral between ends; that, in so far as the achievement of *any* end is dependent on scarce means, it is germane to the preoccupations of the Economist. Economics is not concerned with ends as such. It assumes that human beings have ends in the sense that they have tendencies to conduct which can be defined and understood,[2] and it asks how their

---

[1] The following sections are devoted to the elucidation of the implications of Economics as a positive science. On the question whether Economics should aspire to a normative status, see Chapter VI., Section 4, below.

[2] Such a definition, it will be noticed, entirely removes our conception of an "end" from the realms of the metaphysical. The metaphysical conception of a unitary end of conduct may or may not be valid. In economic analysis we are not concerned with these ultimates. We are concerned simply with the objectives which are, so to speak, formulated in the various tendencies to action. It is not denied that difficulties may arise when the

23

progress towards their objectives is conditioned by the scarcity of means—how the disposal of the scarce means is contingent on these ultimate valuations.

It should be clear, therefore, that to speak of any end as being itself "economic" is entirely misleading. The habit, prevalent among certain groups of economists, of discussing "economic satisfactions" is alien to the central intention of economic analysis. A satisfaction is to be conceived as an end-product of activity. It is not itself part of that activity which we study. It would be going too far to urge that it is impossible to conceive of "economic satisfactions". For, presumably, we *can* so describe a satisfaction which is contingent on the availability of scarce means as distinct from a satisfaction which depends entirely on subjective factors—*e.g.*, the satisfaction of having a summer holiday, as compared with the satisfaction of remembering it. But since, as we have seen, the scarcity of means is so wide as to influence in some degree almost all kinds of conduct, this does not seem a useful conception. And since it is manifestly out of harmony with the main implications of our definition, it is probably better avoided altogether.

It follows, further, that the belief, prevalent among the more neurotic critics of Economic Science, that the preoccupation of the economist is with a peculiarly low type of conduct, depends upon misapprehension. The economist is not concerned with ends as such. He is concerned with the way in which the attainment of ends is limited. The ends may be noble or they may be base. They may be "material" or "immaterial"

formulation is collective, *e.g.* in the sphere of public expenditure. There will be something to be said about this later on. At the moment, all that is necessary is that the limitations of our conception of an end should be recognised.

—if ends can be so described. But if the attainment of one set of ends involves the sacrifice of others, then it has an economic aspect.

All this is quite obvious if only we consider the actual sphere of application of economic analysis, instead of resting content with the assertions of those who do not know what economic analysis is. Suppose, for instance, a community of sybarites, their pleasures gross and sensual, their intellectual activities pre-occupied with the "purely material". It is clear enough that economic analysis can provide categories for describing the relationships between these ends and the means which are available for achieving them. But it is not true, as Ruskin and Carlyle and suchlike critics have asserted, that it is *limited* to this sort of thing. Let us suppose this reprehensible community to be visited by a Savonarola. Their former ends become revolting to them. The pleasures of the senses are banished. The sybarites become ascetics. Surely economic analysis is still applicable. There is no need to change the categories of explanation. All that has happened is that the demand schedules have changed. Some things have become relatively less scarce, others more so. The rent of vineyards falls. The rent of quarries for ecclesiastical masonry rises. That is all. The distribution of time between prayer and good works has its economic aspect equally with the dis-tribution of time between orgies and slumber. The "pig-philosophy"—to use poor Carlyle's name for Economics—turns out to be all-embracing.

To be perfectly fair, it must be admitted that this is a case in which Economists are to some extent to blame for their own misfortunes. As we have seen already, their practice has been unexceptionable.

But their definitions have been misleading, and their attitude in the face of criticism has been unnecessarily apologetic. It is even said that quite modern Economists who have been convinced both of the importance of Economics *and* of its preoccupation with the "more material side of human welfare" have been reduced to prefacing their lectures on general Economic Theory with the rather sheepish apology that, after all, bread and butter are necessary, even to the lives of artists and saints. This seems to be unnecessary in itself, and at the same time liable to give rise to misconception in the minds of those who are apt to find the merely material rather small beer. Nevertheless, if Carlyle and Ruskin had been willing to make the intellectual effort necessary to assimilate the body of analysis bequeathed by the great men whom they criticised so unjustly, they would have realised its profound significance in regard to the interpretation of conduct in general, even if they had been unable to provide any better description than its authors. But, as is abundantly clear from their criticisms, they never made this effort. They did not want to make the effort. It was so much easier, so much more congenial, misrepresenting those who did. And the opportunities for misrepresenting a science that had hardly begun to become conscious of its ultimate implications were not far to seek.

But, if there is no longer any excuse for the detractors of Economics to accuse it of preoccupation with particularly low ends of conduct, there is equally no excuse for Economists to adopt an attitude of superiority as regards the subjects that they are capable of handling. We have already noticed Professor Cannan's rather paradoxical attitude to a

Political Economy of War. And, speaking generally
in this respect, Professor Cannan is a little apt to
follow St. Peter and cry, "Lord, I have never touched
the unclean thing". In the opening chapter of *Wealth*,[1]
he goes out of his way to say that "the criterion of
buying and selling brings many things into economics
which are not commonly treated there and which it
does not seem convenient to treat there. A large trade
has existed since history began in supplying certain
satisfactions of a sensual character which are never
regarded as economic goods. Indulgences to commit
what would otherwise be regarded as offences against
religion or morality have been sold sometimes openly
and at all times under some thin disguise: nobody has
regarded these as economic goods". This is surely
very questionable. Economists, equally with other
human beings, may regard the services of prostitutes
as conducive to no "good" in the ultimate ethical
sense. But to deny that such services are scarce in
the sense in which we use the term, and that there is
therefore an economic aspect of hired love, susceptible
to treatment in the same categories of general analysis
as enable us to explain fluctuations in the price of
hired writing, does not seem to be in accordance with
the facts. As for the sale of indulgences, surely the
status in Economic History of these agreeable transactions is not seriously open to question. Did the
sale of indulgences affect the distribution of income,
the magnitude of expenditure on other commodities,
the direction of production, or did it not? We must
not evade the consequences of the conclusion that all
conduct coming under the influence of scarcity has
its economic aspect.

[1] First edition, p. 15.

3. A very interesting example of the difficulties which may arise if the implications which we have been trying to drag into the light are neglected, is afforded in Sir Josiah Stamp's paper on *Æsthetics as an Economic Factor*.[1] Sir Josiah, who has done so much to maintain sweetness and light in our times, is anxious to preserve the countryside and to safeguard ancient monuments. (The occasion of the paper was a decision on the part of his railway company not to destroy Stratford House, a sixteenth-century half-timbered building in Birmingham, to make room for railway sidings.) At the same time, he believes that Economics is concerned with material welfare.[2] He is, therefore, driven to argue that "indifference to the æsthetic will in the long run lessen the economic product; that attention to the æsthetic will increase economic welfare".[3] That is to say, that if we seek first the Kingdom of the Beautiful, all material welfare will be added unto us. And he brings all the solid weight of his authority to the task of stampeding the business world into believing that this is true.

It is easy to sympathise with the intention of the argument. But it is difficult to believe that its logic is very convincing. It may be perfectly true, as Sir Josiah contends, that the wide interests fostered by the study of ancient monuments and the contemplation of beautiful objects are both stimulating to the intelligence and restful to the nervous system, and that, to that extent, a community which offers opportunities for such interests may gain in other, "more

[1] *Some Economic Factors in Modern Life*, pp. 1-25.
[2] ". . . I use . . . economics as a term to cover the getting of material welfare" (*op. cit.*, p. 3).
[3] *Ibid.*, p. 4.

material", ways. But it is surely an optimism, un-justified either by experience or by a priori probability, to assume that this necessarily follows. It is surely a fact which we must all recognise that rejection of material comfort in favour of æsthetic or ethical values does not necessarily bring material compensation. There are cases when it is either bread or a lily. Choice of the one involves sacrifice of the other, and, although we may be satisfied with our choice, we cannot delude ourselves that it was not really a choice at all, that more bread will follow. It is not true that all things work together for material good to them that love God. So far from postulating a harmony of ends in this sense, Economics brings into full view that conflict of choice which is one of the permanent characteristics of human existence. Your economist is a true tragedian.

What has happened, of course, is that adherence to the "materialist" definition has prevented Sir Josiah from recognising clearly that Economics and Æsthetics are not in pari materia.[1] Æsthetics is concerned with certain kinds of ends. The Æsthetic is an end which offers itself for choice in competition, so to speak, with others. Economics is not concerned at all with any ends as such. It is concerned with ends in so far as they affect the disposition of means. It takes the ends as given in scales of relative valuation, and enquires what consequences follow in regard to certain aspects of behaviour.

But, it may be argued, is it not possible to regard the procuring of money as something which competes

---

[1] It is only fair to state that there are passages in the same essay which seem to be dictated by this sort of consideration. I refer especially to the remarks on pp. 14-16 on balance in consumption. Needless to say, my dispute with Sir Josiah is largely on a matter of presentation.

with other ends, and, if this is so, may we not legitimately speak of an "economic" end of conduct?
This raises questions of very great import. Full discussion of the part played in Economic Analysis of
the assumption that money-making is the sole motive
of conduct must be deferred until a later chapter,
where it will be investigated fully. But, for the
moment, it may be replied that the objection rests
upon a misconception of the significance of money.
Money-making in the normal sense of the term is
merely the intermediate stage between a sale and a
purchase. The procuring of a flow of money from the
sale of one's services or the hiring out of one's property
is not an end *per se*. The money is clearly a means to
ultimate purchase. It is sought, not for itself, but for
the things on which it may be spent—whether these
be the constituents of real income now or of real
income in the future. Money-making in this sense
means securing the means for the achievement of *all*
those ends which are capable of achievement by the
aid of purchasable commodities. Money *as such* is
obviously merely a means—a medium of exchange,
an instrument of calculation. For society, from the
static point of view, the presence of more or less money
is irrelevant. For the individual it is relevant only
in so far as it serves his ultimate objectives. Only the
miser, the psychological monstrosity, desires an infinite accumulation of money. Indeed, so little do we
regard this as typical that, far from regarding the
demand for money to hold as being indefinitely great,
we are in the habit of assuming that money is desired
only to be passed on. Instead of assuming the demand
curve for money to hold to be a straight line parallel
with the y axis, economists have been in the habit

of assuming, as a first approximation, that it is of the nature of a rectangular hyperbola.[1]

4. Economics, then, is in no way to be conceived as we may conceive Ethics or Æsthetics as being concerned with ends as such. It is equally important that its preoccupations should be sharply distinguished from those of the technical arts of production. This raises certain issues of considerable complexity which it is desirable to examine at some length.

The relation between Economics and the technical arts of production is one which has always presented great difficulties to those economists who have thought that they were concerned with the causes of material welfare. It is clear that the technical arts of production are concerned with material welfare. Yet the distinction between art and science does not seem to exhaust the difference. So much scientific knowledge is germane to the technical arts of production that is foreign to Economic Science. Yet where is one to draw the line? Sir William Beveridge has put this difficulty very clearly in his lecture on *Economics as a Liberal Education*. "It is too wide a definition to speak of Economics as the science of the material side of human welfare. A house contributes to human welfare and should be material. If, however, one is considering the building of a house, the question whether the roof should be made of paper or of some other material is a question not of Economics but of

---

[1] On all this, see Wicksteed, *The Commonsense of Political Economy*, pp. 155-157. It is not denied that the acquisition of the power to procure real income may itself become an objective, or that, if it does, the economic system will not be affected in various ways. All that is contended is that to label any of these ends "economic" implies a false view of what is necessarily embraced by economic analysis. Economics takes all ends for granted. They "show" themselves in the scales of relative valuation which are assumed by the propositions of modern economic analysis.

the technique of house building".[1] Nor do we meet this difficulty by inserting the word "general" before "causes of material welfare". Economics is not the aggregate of the technologies. Nor is it an attempt to select from each the elements common to several. Motion study, for instance, may yield generalisations applicable to more than one occupation. But motion study has nothing to do with Economics. Nor, in spite of the hopes of certain industrial psychologists, is it capable of taking its place.[2] So long as we remain within the ambit of any definition of the subject-matter of Economics in terms of the causes of material welfare, the connection between Economics and the technical arts of production must remain hopelessly obscure.

But, from the point of view of the definition we have adopted, the connection is perfectly definite. The technical arts of production are simply to be grouped among the *given* factors influencing the relative scarcity of different economic goods.[2] The technique of cotton manufacture, as such, is no part of the subject-matter of Economics, but the existence of a given technique of various potentialities, together with the other factors influencing supply, conditions the possible response to any valuation of cotton goods, and consequently influences the adaptations which it is the business of Economics to study.

[1] *Economica*, vol. i., p. 3. Of course the question whether the roof shall be of slate or tiles, for instance, may well depend on the relative prices of these materials and therefore have an economic aspect. Technique merely prescribes certain limits within which choice may operate. See below, p. 35.

[2] An eminent industrial psychologist once genially assured me that "if people only understood industrial psychology there would be no need for Economics". With considerable interest, I at once enquired his solution of a problem of foreign exchange which had been perplexing me, but to my great mortification no answer was forthcoming.

So far, matters are supremely simple. But now it is necessary to remove certain possible misunderstandings. At first sight it might appear as if the conception we are adopting ran the danger of tipping the baby out with the bath water. In regarding technique as providing merely given data, are we not excluding from the subject-matter of Economics just those matters where economic analysis is most at home? For is not production a matter of technique? And is not the Theory of Production one of the central preoccupations of economic analysis?

The objection sounds plausible. But, in fact, it involves a complete misapprehension—a misapprehension which it is important finally to dispel. The attitude we have adopted towards the technical arts of production does not eliminate the desirability of an economic theory of production.[1] For the influences determining the structure of production are not purely technical in nature. No doubt, technique is very important. But technique is not everything. It is one of the merits of modern analysis that it enables us to put technique in its proper place. This deserves further elucidation. It is not an exaggeration to say that, at the present day, one of the main dangers to civilisation arises from the inability of minds trained in the natural sciences to perceive the difference between the economic and the technical.

Let us consider the behaviour of an isolated man in disposing of a single scarce commodity.[2] Let us consider, for instance, the behaviour of a Robinson

---

[1] Whether this theory is to be conceived, as it sometimes has been in the past, as concerned with aggregates of wealth is another matter which will be dealt with in the next chapter. See below, Chapter III., Section 6.

[2] Compare Oswalt, *Vorträge über wirtschaftliche Grundbegriffe*, pp. 20-41.

Crusoe in regard to a stock of wood of strictly limited dimensions. Robinson has not sufficient wood for all the purposes to which he could put it. For the time being the stock is irreplaceable. What are the influences which will determine the way in which he utilises it?

Now, if the wood can only be used at one time and for one purpose, or if it is only wanted at one time and for one purpose, and if we assume that Robinson has ample time to devote to its utilisation, it is perfectly true that his economising will be dictated entirely by his knowledge of the technical arts of production concerned. If he only wants the wood to make a fire of given dimensions, then, if there is only a limited supply of wood available, his activities will be determined by his knowledge of the technique of fire-making. His activities in this respect are purely technical.

But if he wants the wood for more than one purpose—if, in addition to wanting it for a fire, he needs it for fencing the ground round the cabin and keeping the fence in good condition—then, inevitably, he is confronted by a new problem—*the problem of how much wood to use for fires and how much for fencing.* In these circumstances the techniques of fire-making and fencing are still important. But the problem is no longer a purely technical problem. Or, to put the matter in more behaviouristic terms, the influences on his disposal of wood are no longer purely technical. Conduct is the resultant of conflicting psychological pulls acting within an environment of given material and technical possibilities. The problem of technique and the problem of economy are fundamentally different problems. To use Professor Mayer's very elegant way of putting the distinction, the problem of technique arises when there is one end and a multiplicity of means, the problem of economy when both the ends and the means are multiple.[1]

Now, as we have seen already, it is one of the characteristics of the world as we find it that our ends are various and that most of the scarce means at our disposal are capable of alternative application. This applies not only to scarce products. It applies still more to the ultimate factors of production. The various kinds of natural resources and labour can be used for an almost infinite variety of purposes. The disposition to abstain from consumption in the present releases uses of primary factors for more than one kind of roundabout process. And, for this reason, a mere knowledge of existing technique does not enable us to determine the actual "set" of the productive apparatus. We need to know also the ultimate valuations of the producers and consumers connected with it. It is out of the interplay of the given systems of ends on the one side and the material and technical potentialities on the other, that the aspects of behaviour which the economist studies are determined.

All this sounds very abstract. But, in fact, it merely states, in terms of a degree of generality appropriate to the very fundamental questions we are examining, facts which are well known to all of us. If we ask the concrete question, why is the production of such a commodity in such and such an area what it is, and not something else, our answer is not couched in terms which, in the first instance, have a technical implication. Our answer runs in terms of prices and

---

[1] See Hans Mayer, *op. cit.*, pp. 5 and 6.

costs; and, as every first-year student knows, prices and costs are the reflection of relative valuations, not of merely technical conditions. We all know of commodities which, from the technical point of view, could be produced quite easily.[1] Yet their production is not at the moment a business proposition. Why is this? Because, given the probable price, the costs involved are too great. And why are costs too great? Because the technique is not sufficiently developed? This is only true in a historical sense. But it does not answer the fundamental question why, *given the technique*, the costs are too high. And the answer to that can only be couched in economic terms. It depends essentially on the price which it is necessary to pay for the factors of production involved compared with the probable price of the product. And that may depend on a variety of considerations. In competitive conditions, it will depend on the valuations placed by consumers on the commodities which the factors are capable of producing. And if the costs are too high, that means that the factors of production can be employed elsewhere producing commodities which are valued more highly. If the supply of any factor is monopolised, then high costs may merely mean that the controllers of the monopoly are pursuing a policy which leads to some of the factors they control being temporarily unemployed. But, in any case, the process of ultimate explanation begins just where the description of the technical conditions leaves off.

But this brings us back—although with new knowledge of its implications—to the proposition from which we started. Economists are not interested in

[1] The production of motor oils from coal is a very topical case in point.

technique as such. They are interested in it solely as one of the influences determining relative scarcity. Conditions of technique "show" themselves in the productivity functions just as conditions of taste "show" themselves in the scales of relative valuations. But there the connection ceases. Economics is a study of the disposal of scarce commodities. The technical arts of production study the "intrinsic" properties of objects or human beings.[1]

5. It follows from the argument of the preceding sections that the subject-matter of Economics is essentially a relationship—a relationship between ends conceived as tendencies to conduct, on the one hand, and the technical and social environment on the other. Ends as such do not form part of this subject-matter. Nor does the technical and social environment. It is the relationships between these things and not the things in themselves which are important for the economist.

If this point of view be accepted, a far-reaching elucidation of the nature of Economic History and what is sometimes called Descriptive Economics is possible—an elucidation which renders clear the relationship between these branches of study and theoretical Economics and removes all possible grounds of conflict between them. The nature of Economic Theory is clear. It is the study of the formal implications of this relationship of ends and means. The nature of Economic History should be no less evident. It is the study of the substantial instances in which this relationship shows itself through time. It is the explanation of the historical

[1] On the general question of the relation between technology and Economics, see Mises, *Vom Weg der Subjectiv Wertlehre* (*Schriften des Vereins für Sozialpolitik*, Bd. 183, pp. 83-84).

manifestations of "scarcity". Economic Theory describes the forms, Economic History the substance.
Thus, in regard to Economic History no more
than in regard to Economic Theory can we classify
events into groups and say: these are the subject-
matter of your branch of knowledge and these are not.
The province of Economic History, equally with the
province of Economic Theory, cannot be restricted
to any part of the stream of events without doing
violence to its inner intentions. But no more than
any other kind of history does it attempt comprehensive description of this stream of events;[1] it concen-
trates solely upon the description of a certain *aspect*
thereof—a changing network of economic relationships,[2] the effect on values in the economic sense of
changes in ends and changes in the technical and social
opportunities of realising them.[3]

---

[1] On the impossibility of history of any kind without selective principle
see Rickert, *Kulturwissenschaft und Naturwissenschaft*, pp. 28-60.
[2] Cp. Cunningham: "Economic History is not so much the study of a
special class of facts as the study of all the facts from a special point of
view" (*Growth of English Industry and Commerce*, vol. i., p. 8).
[3] On the relation between Economic Theory and Economic History,
see Hecksher, *A Plea for Theory in Economic History* (*Economic History*,
vol. i., pp. 525-535); Clapham, *The Study of Economic History, passim*;
Mises, *Soziologie und Geschichte* (*Archiv für Sozialwissenschaft und Sozialpolitik*, Bd. 61, pp. 465-512). It may be urged that the above description
of the nature of Economic History presents a very idealised picture of what
is to be found in the average work on Economic History. And it may be
admitted that, in the past, Economic History, equally with Economic Theory,
has not always succeeded in purging itself of adventitious elements. In
particular it is clear that the influence of the German Historical School was
responsible for the intrusion of all sorts of sociological and ethical elements
which cannot, by the widest extension of the meaning of words, be described
as *Economic* History. It is true too that there has been considerable confusion between Economic History and the economic interpretation of other
aspects of history—in the sense of the word "economic" suggested above
—and between Economic History and the "Economic Interpretation" of
History in the sense of the Materialist Interpretation of History (see below,
Section 6). But the main stream of Economic History from Fleetwood and
Adam Smith down to Professor Clapham bears the interpretation put on it
here more consistently than any other.

A few illustrations should make this clear. Let us take, for example, that vast upheaval which, for the sake of compendious description, we call the Reformation. From the point of view of the historian of religion, the Reformation is significant in its influence on doctrine and ecclesiastical organisation. From the point of view of the political historian, its interest consists in the changes in political organisation, the new relations of rulers and subjects, the emergence of the national states, to which it gave rise. To the cultural historian it signifies important changes both in the form and the subject-matter of the arts, and the freeing of the spirit of modern scientific enquiry. But to the economic historian it signifies chiefly changes in the distribution of property, changes in the channels of trade, changes in the demand for fish, changes in the supply of indulgences, changes in the incidence of taxes. The economic historian is not interested in the changes of ends and the changes of means in themselves. He is interested only in so far as they affect the series of relationships between means and ends which it is his function to study.

Again, we may take a change in the technical processes of production—the invention of the steam engine or the discovery of rail transport. Events of this sort, equally with changes in ends, have an almost inexhaustible variety of aspects. They are significant for the history of technique, for the history of manners, for the history of the arts, and so on *ad infinitum*. But, for the economic historian, all these aspects are irrelevant save in so far as they involve action and reaction in his sphere of interest. The precise shape of the early steam engine and the physical principles upon which it rested are no concern of the

economic historian as economic historian—although
economic historians in the past have often displayed
a quite inordinate interest in such matters. For him
it is significant because it affected the supply of and
the demand for certain products and certain factors
of production, because it affected the price and income
structures of the communities where it was adopted.

So, too, in the field of "Descriptive Economics"—
the Economic History of the present day—the main
object is always the elucidation of particular "scarcity
relationships"—although the attainment of this object
often necessarily involves very specialised investigations. In the study of monetary phenomena, for
instance, we are often compelled to embark upon
enquiries of a highly technical or legal character—
the mode of granting overdrafts, the law relating to
the issue of paper money. For the banker or the
lawyer these things are the focus of attention. But
for the economist, although an exact knowledge of
them may be essential to his purpose, the acquisition
of this knowledge is essentially subservient to his
main purpose of explaining the potentialities, in particular situations, of changes in the supply of circulating
media. The technical and the legal are of interest
solely in so far as they have this aspect.[1]

[1] Considerations of this sort suggest the very real dangers of overmuch
sectionalism in economic studies. In recent years there has been an immense
extension of sectional studies in the economic field. We have institutes of
Agricultural Economics, Transport Economics, Mining Economics, and so
on. Sombart gives a list of some sixty special connections (including *Schweine-*
and *Vieh-*) in which the word *Wirtschaft*, the German equivalent for our
Economics, has acquired some sense (*Die Drei Nationalökonomien*, p. 17).
And, no doubt, up to a point this is all to the good. In the realm of Applied
Economics, some division of labour is essential, and, as we shall see later,
theory cannot be fruitfully applied to the interpretation of concrete situations unless it is informed continually of the changing background of the
facts of particular industries. But, as experience shows, sectional investigations conducted in isolation are exposed to very grave dangers. If continual

6. Finally, we may notice the bearing of all this on the celebrated Materialist or "Economic" Interpretation of History. For, from the point of view we have adopted, certain distinctions, not always clearly recognised, are discernible.

We have seen already that, although in the past Economics has been given what may be described as a "materialist" definition, yet its content is not at all materialistic. The change of definition which we have suggested, so far from necessitating a change of content, serves only to make the present content more comprehensible. The "materialism" of Economics was a pseudo-materialism. In fact, it is not materialistic at all.

It might be thought that a similar state of affairs prevailed in regard to the "Economic" or Materialist Interpretation of History—that a mere change of label would suffice to make this doctrine consistent with the modern conception of economic analysis. But this is not so. For the so-called "Economic" Interpretation of History is not only *labelled* "Materialist", it is *in substance* through and through materialistic. It holds that all the events of history, or at any rate

vigilance is not exercised they tend to the gradual replacement of economic by technological interests. The focus of attention becomes shifted, and a body of generalisations which have only technical significance comes to masquerade under the garb of Economic Science. And this is fatal. For, since the scarcity of means is relative to *all* ends, it follows that an adequate view of the influences governing social relationships in their economic aspects can only be obtained by viewing the economic system as a whole. In the economic system, "industries" do not live to themselves. Their *raison d'être*, indeed, is the existence of other industries, and their fortunes can only be understood in relation to the whole network of economic relationships. It follows, therefore, that studies which are exclusively devoted to one industry or occupation are continually exposed to the danger of losing touch with the essentials. Their attention may be supposed to be directed to the study of prices and costs, but they tend continually to degenerate either into mere accountancy or into amateur technology. This may or may not be interesting or useful, but it has little to do with Economic Science.

all the major events in history, are attributable to "material" changes, not in the philosophical sense that these events are part of the material world, nor in the psychological sense that psychic dispositions are the mere epiphenomena of physiological changes— though, of course, Marx would have accepted these positions—but in the sense that the material technique of production conditions the form of all social institutions, and all changes in social institutions are the result of changes in the technique of production. History is the epiphenomenon of technical change. The history of tools is the history of mankind.[1]

Now, whether this doctrine is right or wrong, it is certainly materialistic, and it is certainly not derivative from Economic Science as we know it. It asserts quite definitely, not only that technical changes cause changes in scarcity relationships and social institutions generally—which would be a proposition in harmony with modern economic analysis—but also that all changes in social relations are due to technical changes—which is a sociological proposition quite outside the limited range of Economic generalisation. It definitely implies that all changes in ends, in relative

---

[1] It is extremely difficult to give a compendious account of this doctrine, for its advocates will not allow themselves to be pinned down to precise definition. This is not surprising, since it is obvious that their whole conception of historical causation is hopelessly naïve and muddled.

In what follows, the distinctions I employ are very similar to those used by Dr. Strigl (*op. cit.*, pp. 158-161). The differences in our emphasis may be attributed to a difference of expository purpose. Dr. Strigl is trying to exhibit the Materialist Interpretation as a primitive theory of what he calls *Datenänderung*. He, therefore, tends to slur its deficiency in refusing to take account of changes in ultimate valuations save as derivative from changes on the supply side. I am anxious to show the fundamental distinction between any explanation of history springing from economic analysis as we know it and the explanation attempted by the Materialist Interpretation. I therefore drag this particular point into the light. I do not think that Dr. Strigl would question the logic of my distinctions any more than I would question the interest of his analogy.

valuations, are conditioned by changes in the technical potentialities of production. It implies, that is to say, that ultimate valuations are merely the bye-product of technical conditions. If technical conditions alter, tastes, etc., alter. If they remain unchanged, then tastes, etc., are unaltered. There are no *autonomous* changes on the demand side. What changes occur are, in the end, attributable to changes in the technical machinery of supply. There is no independent "psychological" (or, for that matter, "physiological") side to scarcity. No matter what their fundamental make-up, be it inherited or acquired, men in similar technical environments will develop similar habits and institutions. This may be right or wrong, pseudo-Hegelian twaddle or profound insight into things which at the moment are certainly not susceptible of scientific analysis, but it is not to be deduced from any laws of theoretical Economics. It is a general statement about the causation of human motive which, from the point of view of Economic Science, is sheer metaphysics. The label "Materialist" fits the doctrine. The label "Economic" is misplaced. Economics may well provide an important instrument for the elucidation of history. But there is nothing in economic analysis which entitles us to assert that all history is to be explained in "economic" terms, if "economic" is to be used as equivalent to the technically material. The Materialist Interpretation of History has come to be called the Economic Interpretation of History, because it was thought that the subject-matter of Economics was "the causes of material welfare". Once it is realised that this is not the case, the Materialist Interpretation must stand or fall by itself. Economic Science lends no support to its doctrines. Nor does it assume at any point the connections it asserts. From the point of view of Economic Science, changes in relative valuations are given data.[1]

[1] It might be argued, indeed, that a thorough understanding of economic analysis was conducive to presumptions against the Materialist Interpretation. Once it is realised how changes in technique *directly* influence the amounts demanded, it is extraordinarily difficult to bring oneself to postulate any *necessary* connection between technical changes and autonomous changes on the demand side. Such an attitude of scepticism towards the Marxian theory does not imply denial of metaphysical materialism—though equally it does not imply its acceptance—it implies merely a refusal to believe that the causes influencing taste and so on are technical in nature. The most intransigent behaviourist need find nothing to quarrel with in the belief that technical materialism in this sense is a very misleading half truth.

CHAPTER III

THE RELATIVITY OF ECONOMIC " QUANTITIES "

1. THAT aspect of behaviour which is the subject-matter of Economics is, as we have seen, conditioned by the scarcity of *given* means for the attainment of *given* ends. It is clear, therefore, that the quality of scarcity in goods is not an "absolute" quality. Scarcity does not mean mere infrequency of occurrence. It means limitation in relation to demand. Good eggs are scarce because, having regard to the demand for them, there are not enough to go round. But bad eggs, of which, let us hope, there are far fewer in existence, are not scarce at all in our sense. They are redundant. This conception of scarcity has implications both for theory and for practice which it is the object of this chapter to elucidate.

2. It follows from what has just been said that the conception of an economic good is necessarily purely formal.[1] There is no quality in things taken out of their relation to men which can make them economic goods. There is no quality in services taken

---

[1] Of course, the conceptions of any pure science are *necessarily* purely formal. If we were attempting to construct Economics from pure logic instead of describing it as it appears from a consideration of what is essential in its subject-matter, this would be a guiding consideration. But it is interesting to observe how, starting from the inspection of an apparatus for solving concrete problems, we eventually arrive, by the necessities of accurate description, at conceptions which are in full conformity with the expectations of pure methodology.

out of relation to the end served which makes them economic. Whether a particular thing or a particular service is an economic good depends entirely on its relation to valuations. Thus wealth[1] is not wealth because of its substantial qualities. It is wealth because it is scarce. We cannot define wealth in physical terms as we can define food in terms of vitamin content or calorific value. It is an essentially relative concept. For the community of ascetics discussed in the last chapter there may be so many goods of certain kinds in relation to the demand for them that they are free goods— not wealth at all in the strict sense. In similar circumstances, the community of sybarites might be "poor". That is to say, for them, the self-same goods might be economic goods.

So, too, when we think of productive power in the economic sense, we do not mean something absolute —something capable of physical computation. We mean power to satisfy given demands. If the given demands change, then productive power in this sense changes also.

A very vivid example of what this means is to be found in Mr. Winston Churchill's account of the situation confronting the Ministry of Munitions at 11 a.m. on November 11th, 1918—the moment of the signing of the Armistice. After years of effort, the nation had acquired a machine for turning out the

[1] The term wealth is used here as equivalent to a flow of economic goods. But I think it is clear that there are profound disadvantages in using it in this sense. It would be very paradoxical to have to maintain that, if "economic" goods by reason of multiplication became "free" goods, wealth would diminish. Yet that might be urged to the implication of this usage. Hence, in any rigid delimitation of Economics, the term wealth should be avoided. It is used here simply in elucidation of the implications for everyday discussion of the somewhat remote propositions of the preceding paragraph.

materials of war in unprecedented quantities. Enormous programmes of production were in every stage of completion. Suddenly the whole position is changed. The "demand" collapses. The needs of war are at an end. What was to be done? Mr. Churchill relates how, in the interests of a smooth change-over, instructions were issued that material more than 60 per cent. advanced was to be finished. "Thus for many weeks after the war was over we continued to disgorge upon the gaping world masses of artillery and military materials of every kind."[1] "It was waste", he adds, "but perhaps it was a prudent waste." Whether this last contention is correct or not is irrelevant to the point under discussion. What is relevant is that what at 10.55 a.m. that morning was wealth and productive power, at 11.5 had become "not-wealth," an embarrassment, a source of social waste. The substance had not changed. The guns were the same. The potentialities of the machines were the same. From the point of view of the technician, everything was exactly the same. But from the point of view of the economist, everything was different. Guns, explosives, lathes, retorts, all had suffered a sea change. The ends had changed. The scarcity of means was different.[2]

---

[1] *The World Crisis*, vol. v., pp. 33-35.

[2] It is, perhaps, worth while observing how our practice here differs from the practice which would seem to follow from Professor Cannan's procedure. Having defined wealth as material welfare, Professor Cannan would be logically compelled to argue that we were not producing during the War. In fact, he gets out of the difficulty by arguing that we may say that we were producing produce but not material welfare (*Review of Economic Theory*, p. 51). From the point of view of the definitions here adopted, it follows, not that we were not producing, but simply that we were not producing for the same demands as during peace time. From either point of view, the *non-comparability* of material statistics of war and peace follows clearly. But from our point of view the *persistence* of formal economic laws is much more clearly emphasised.

3. The proposition which we have just been discussing, concerning what may be described as the
relativity of "economic quantities", has an important
bearing on many problems of applied Economics—
so important, indeed, that it is worth while, here and
now, interrupting the course of our main argument in
order to examine them rather more fully. There can
be no better illustration of the way in which the
propositions of pure theory facilitate comprehension
of the meaning of concrete issues.

A conspicuous instance of a type of problem
which can only be satisfactorily solved with the aid
of the distinctions we have been developing, is to be
found in contemporary discussions of the alleged
economies of mass production. At the present day
the lay mind is dominated by the spectacular achievements of mass production. Mass production has become a sort of cure-all, an open sesame. The goggled
eyes of the world turn westward to Ford the deliverer.
He who has gaped longest at the conveyors at Detroit
is hailed as the most competent economist.

Now, naturally, no economist in his senses would
wish to deny the importance for modern civilisation
of the potentialities of modern manufacturing technique. The technical changes which bring to the door,
even of the comparatively poor man, the motor-car,
the gramophone, the wireless apparatus, are truly
momentous changes. But, in judging their significance
in regard to a given set of ends, it is very important
to bear in mind this distinction between the mere
multiplication of material objects and the satisfaction
of demand, which the definitions of this chapter
elucidate. To use a convenient jargon, it is important
to bear in mind the distinction between technical and

value productivity. The mass production of particular things irrespective of demand for them, however technically efficient, is not necessarily "economical". As we have seen already, there is a fundamental difference between technical and economic problems.[1] We may take it as obvious that, within certain limits (which, of course, change with changing conditions of technique), specialisation of men and machinery is conducive to technical efficiency. But the extent to which such specialisation is "economical" depends essentially upon the extent of the market—that is to say, upon demand.[2] For a blacksmith producing for a small and isolated community to specialise solely on the production of a certain type of horse-shoe, in order to secure the economies of mass production, would be folly. After he has made a limited number of shoes of one size, it is clearly better for him to turn his attention to producing shoes of other sizes, additional units of which will be more urgently demanded, than additional units of the size of which he has already manufactured a large quantity.

So, too, in the world at large at any particular moment, there are definite limits to the extent to which the mass production of any one type of commodity to the exclusion of other types is in conformity with the demands of consumers. If it is carried beyond these limits, not only is there waste, in the sense that productive power is used to produce goods of less value than could be produced otherwise, but there is also definite financial loss for the productive enterprise concerned. It is one of the paradoxes of the history of

[1] See above, pp. 31-37.
[2] See Allyn Young, *Increasing Returns and Economic Progress* (*Economic Journal*, vol. xxxviii., pp. 528-542). On the sense in which it is legitimate to use the term "economical" in this connection, see Chapter VI. below.

4

modern thought that, at a time when the disproportionate development of particular lines of production
has wrought more chaos in the economic system than
at any earlier period in history, there should arise the
naïve belief that a general resort to mass production,
whenever and wherever it is technically possible,
regardless of the conditions of demand, will see us out
of our difficulties.[1] It is the nemesis of the worship of
the machine, the paralysis of the intellect of a world
of technicians.

This confusion between technical potentiality and
economic value, which, borrowing a phrase of Professor
Whitehead's, we may call the "fallacy of misplaced
concreteness",[2] also underlies certain notions at
present unduly prevalent with regard to the value
of fixed capital. It is sometimes thought that the
fact that large sums of money have been sunk in
certain forms of fixed capital renders it undesirable,
if consumer's demand changes, or if technical inven-

[1] It is a striking comment on the quality of the intellectual life of our
time that economies of mass production are often invoked as an argument
in favour of the tariffs which are at present strangling trade, on the ground
that "safeguarding the home market" makes possible the desired con-
centration. Quite apart from the logical weakness and ambiguities of the
argument, which are sufficiently exposed in any of the standard works on
the subject (see, *e.g.*, Pigou, *Protective and Preferential Import Duties,*
pp. 16-19), this is a very good example of inability to see the wood for the
trees ! As we have seen already, the wider the market the more extensive is
the resort which is possible to the economies of mass production. Since
tariffs necessarily contract markets, it therefore follows that the growth
of tariffs must prevent resort to the economies of mass production being as
widespread as might otherwise be the case. The leaders of industry all over
the world, deluded by the prospect of a momentary gain, pursue a policy
which in the long run is bound to be inimical to yet greater profits. A
world in which the inhabitants of each petty national area insulate themselves against commercial intercourse with the rest of mankind "to safeguard the home market" is a world in which the genuine economies of large
production which modern technique makes possible are for ever unattain-
able. Yet that is the world which, at the present time, we are all busily
engaged in making.
[2] *Science and the Modern World,* p. 64.

tion renders it possible to satisfy a given consumer's demand in other more profitable ways, that the capital should fall into disuse. If the satisfaction of demand is assumed as the criterion of economic organisation, this belief is completely fallacious. If I purchase a railway ticket from London to Glasgow, and half-way on my journey I receive a telegram informing me that my appointment must take place in Manchester, it is not rational conduct for me to continue my journey northwards, just because I have "sunk capital" in the ticket which I am unable to recover. It is true that the ticket is still as "technically efficient" in procuring me the right to go to Glasgow. But my objective has now changed. The power to continue my journey northward is no longer valuable to me. To continue nevertheless would be irrational. In Economics, as Jevons remarked, bygones are forever bygones.

Exactly similar considerations apply when we are considering the present status of machinery for whose products demand has ceased, or which has ceased to be as profitable, taking everything into account, as other kinds of machinery. Although the machinery may be technically as efficient as it was before these changes, yet its economic status is different.[1] No doubt, *if* the change in demand or in cost conditions which led to its supersession had been foreseen, the disposition of resources would have been different. In that sense it is not meaningless to speak of a waste

[1] Compare Pigou, *Economics of Welfare*, 3rd edition, pp. 190-192. It is, perhaps, worth noting that most contemporary discussion of the so-called Transport Problem completely ignores these elementary considerations. If there is a concealed subsidy to motor transport through public expenditure on roads, this is a matter for the Chancellor of the Exchequer. It is no argument for attempting to make people go by train who prefer to travel by road. If we want to preserve railways which are unprofitable in the present conditions of demand, we should subsidise them as ancient monuments.

due to ignorance. But once the change has taken place, what has happened before is totally irrelevant —it is waste to take it into further consideration. The problem is one of adjustment to the situation that is given. When every legitimate criticism of the Subjective Theory of Value has been taken into account, it still remains the unshakable achievement of this theory that it focuses attention on this fact, as important in applied economics as in the purest of pure theory.

As a last example of the importance for applied economics of the propositions we have been considering, we may examine certain misconceptions with regard to the economic effects of inflation. It is a well-known fact that during periods of inflation there is often for a time extreme activity in the constructional industries. Under the stimulus of the artificially low interest rates, overhauling of capital equipment on the most extensive scale is often undertaken. New factories are built. Old factories are re-equipped. To the lay mind, there is something extraordinarily fascinating about this spectacular activity; and when the effects of inflation are being discussed, it is not infrequently regarded as a virtue that it should be instrumental in bringing this about. How often does one hear it said of the German inflation that, while it was painful enough while it lasted, it did at least provide German industry with a new capital equipment. Indeed, no less an authority than Professor F. B. Graham has given the weight of his authority to this view.[1]

---

[1] *Exchange, Prices and Production in Hyperinflation : Germany*, 1920-1923, p. 320. "So far as output is concerned, there is little support in actual statistics for the contention that the evils of inflation were other than evils of distribution." In his conclusion, Professor Graham does indeed make the

But, plausible as all this may seem, it is founded on the same crude materialist conception as the other fallacies we have been discussing. For the efficiency of any industrial system does not consist in the presence of large quantities of up-to-date capital equipment, irrespective of the demand for its products or the price of the factors of production which are needed for the profitable exploitation of such equipment. It consists in the degree of adaptation to meet demand of the organisation of *all* resources. Now it can be shown[1] that, during times of inflation, the artificially low rates of interest tend to encourage expansion of certain kinds of capitalistic production in such measure that, when the stimulus is exhausted, it is no longer possible to work them as profitable undertakings. At the same time, liquid resources are dissipated and exhausted. When the slump comes, the system is left high and dry with an incubus of fixed capital too costly to be worked at a profit, and a relative shortage of "fluid capital" which causes interest rates to be stringent and oppressive. The beautiful machinery which so impressed the newspaper correspondents is still there, but the wheels are empty of profit. The material is there. But it has lost its economic significance. Considerations of this sort might have been thought to be very remote from reality at the time of the German inflation or at

---

grudging admission that "in the later stages of inflation, investment in durable goods took on a bizarre aspect". But he seems to be under the delusion that the "quality" of capital equipment may deteriorate without any detriment to its "quantity". A better example of the "fallacy of misplaced concreteness" could scarcely be imagined.

[1] See Mises, *Theorie des Geldes und der Umlaufsmittel*, 2nd edition, pp. 347-376; Hayek, *Geldtheorie und Konjunkturtheorie*, and *Prices and Production*; Strigl, *Die Produktion unter dem Einflusse einer Kreditexpansion* (*Schriften des Vereins für Sozialpolitik*, Bd. 173, pp. 187-211).

the time of stabilisation. After years of chronic "capital shortage" in that unhappy country, they begin to appear less paradoxical.[1]

4. It is time to return to more abstract considerations. We have next to consider the bearing of our definitions upon the meaning of Economic Statistics.

Economic Statistics employ two kinds of units of reckoning—physical units and value units. Reckoning is by "weight and tale" or by valuation—so many tons of coal, so many pounds sterling worth of coal. From the point of view of economic analysis, what meaning is to be attached to these computations?

So far as physical reckonings are concerned, what has been said already is sufficient. There is no need further to labour the proposition that, although, as records of fact, physical computations may be unimpeachable and, in certain connections, useful, yet from the point of view of the economist they have no significance apart from relative valuations. No doubt, assuming a certain empirical permanence of relative valuations, many physical series have direct significance for applied Economics. But from the logical point of view this is an accident. The significance of the series always depends upon the background of relative valuation.

So far as reckonings in terms of value are concerned, there are other subtler difficulties which we must now proceed to unravel.

According to modern price theory, the prices of different commodities and factors of production are expressions of relative scarcity, or, in other words, marginal valuations.[2] Given an initial distribution

[1] See Bonn, *Das Schicksal des Deutschen Kapitalismus*, pp. 14-31.

[2] The pretence that there is anything fundamentally different between the various modern versions of the theory of price equilibrium is now

of resources, each individual entering the market may be conceived to have a scale of relative valuations; and the interplay of the market serves to bring these individual scales and the market scale as expressed in relative prices into harmony with one another.[1] Prices, therefore, express in money a grading of the various goods and services coming on the market. Any given price, therefore, has significance only in relation to the other prices prevailing at that time. Taken by itself it means nothing. It is only as the expression in money terms of a certain order of preference that it means anything at all. As Samuel Bailey pointed out over a hundred years ago, "As we cannot speak of the distance of any object without implying some other object between which and the former this relation exists, so we cannot speak of the value of a commodity, but in reference to another commodity compared with it. A thing cannot be valuable in itself without reference to another thing, any more than a thing can be distant in itself without reference to another thing."[2]

It follows from this that the term which, for the sake of continuity and to raise certain definite associations, we have used hitherto in this chapter, the term "economic *quantity*" is really very misleading. A price, it is true, expresses the quantity of money which it is necessary to give in exchange for a given

---

sufficiently exploded to be dispensed with. See Morgenstern, *Die Drei Grundtypen der Theorie des Subjektiven Wertes (Schriften des Vereins für Sozialpolitik*, Bd. 183, 1, pp. 1-42). On the alleged difference of the Casselian system, see Schams, *Die Casselsche Gleichungen und die Mathematische Wirtschaftstheorie, Jahrbücher für Nationalökonomie und Statistik*, Bd. 127, 1927, p. 385; Wicksell, *Professor Cassel's Nationalökonomisches System*; *Schmoller's Jahrbuch*, 52 Jahr, pp. 771-808.

[1] For an exhaustive description of the process, see especially Wicksteed, *Commonsense of Political Economy*, pp. 212-400.

[2] *A Critical Dissertation on Value*, p. 5.

commodity. But its significance is the relationship between this quantity of money and other similar quantities. And the valuations which the price system expresses are not quantities at all. They are arrangements in a certain order. To assume that the scale of relative prices measures any quantity at all save quantities of money is gratuitous metaphysics. Value is a relation, not a measurement.[1]

But, if this is so, it follows that the addition of prices or individual incomes to form social aggregates is an operation with a very limited meaning. As quantities of money expended, particular prices and particular incomes are capable of addition, and the total arrived at has a definite monetary significance. But as expressions of an order of preference, a relative scale, they are incapable of addition. Their aggregate has no meaning. They are only significant in relation to each other. Estimates of the social income have a quite definite meaning for monetary theory. But beyond this they have only *conventional* significance.

It is important to realise exactly both the weight and the limitations of this conclusion. It does mean that a comprehensive aggregate of prices means nothing but a stream of money payments. Both the concept of world money income and the national money income have strict significance only for monetary theory—the one in relation to the general Theory of Indirect Exchange, the other to the Ricardian Theory of

---

[1] See Čuhel, *Zur Lehre der Bedurfnissen*, pp. 186-216. See also Mises, *Theorie des Geldes*, pp. 10-20, and Knight, *Risk, Uncertainty and Profit*, pp. 69 and 70 (footnote). Recognition of the ordinal nature of the valuations implied in price is fundamental. It is difficult to overstress its importance. With one slash of Occam's razor, it extrudes for ever from economic analysis the last vestiges of psychological hedonism. The conception is implicit in Menger's use of the term *Bedeutung* in his statement of the Theory of Value, but the main credit for its explicit statement and subsequent elaboration is due to subsequent writers.

the Distribution of the Precious Metals. But, of course, this does not exclude a *conventional* significance. If we like to assume that preferences and property do not change rapidly within short periods, and that certain price changes may be regarded as particularly significant for the majority of economic subjects, then no doubt we may assign to the movements of these aggregates a certain arbitrary meaning which is not without its uses. And this is all that is claimed for such estimates by the best statisticians. All that is intended here is to emphasise the essentially arbitrary nature of the assumptions necessary. They do not have an exact counterpart in fact, and they do not follow from the main categories of pure theory.

We can see the bearing of all this if we consider for a moment the use which may be made of such aggregates in examining the probable effects of drastic changes in distribution. From time to time computations are made of the total money income accruing within a given area, and, from these totals, attempts are made to estimate the effects of large changes in an equilitarian direction. The best known of such attempts are the estimates of Professor Bowley and Sir Josiah Stamp.[1]

Now, in so far as such estimates are confined to ascertaining the initial amount of spending power available for redistribution, they are valuable and important. And, of course, this is all that has ever been contended by the distinguished statisticians who put them forward. But beyond this it is futile to attach any precise significance to them. For, by the very fact of redistribution, relative valua-

---

[1] See Bowley, *The Division of the Product of Industry*, and Stamp, *Wealth and Taxable Capacity*.

tions would necessarily alter. The whole "set" of the productive machine would be different. The stream of goods and services would have a different composition. Indeed, if we think a little further into the problem, we can see that an estimate of this sort must very grossly overestimate the amount of productive power that would be released by such changes. For a substantial proportion of the high incomes of the rich are due to the existence of other rich persons. Lawyers, doctors, the proprietors of rare sites, etc., enjoy high incomes because there exist people with high incomes who value their services highly. Redistribute money incomes, and, although the technical efficiency of the factors concerned would be the same, their place on the relative scale would be entirely different. With a constant volume of money and a constant velocity of circulation, it is almost certain that the main initial result would be a rise in the prices of articles of working-class consumption. This conclusion, which is obvious enough from the census of occupations, tends actually to be concealed by computations in money—pessimistic as these computations are often supposed to be. If we compute the proportion of the population now producing real income for the rich who could be turned to producing real income for the poor, it is easy to see that the increase available would be negligible. If we attempt greater precision by means of money computations, we are likely to exaggerate. And the greater the degree of initial inequality, the greater the degree of exaggeration.[1]

[1] Of course, this is not necessarily so. If, instead of spending their incomes on the expensive services of doctors, lawyers, and so on, the rich were in the habit of spending them on vast retinues of retainers *who were supported by the efforts of others*, the change in money incomes might release factors which, from the point of view of the new conditions of demand, represented much productive power. But in fact this is not the case. Even

5. It is a further consequence of the conception of value as an expression of an order of preference that comparisons of prices have no precise significance, unless exchange is possible between the commodities whose prices are being compared.

It follows, therefore, that to compare the prices of a particular commodity at different periods of time in the past, is an operation which, by itself, does not necessarily afford results which have further meaning. The fact that bread last year was 8d. and bread this year is 6d. does not necessarily imply that the relative scarcity of bread this year is less than the relative scarcity of bread last year. The significant comparison is not the comparison between 8d. last year and 6d. this year, but the comparison between 8d. and other prices last year and the comparison between 6d. and other prices this year. For it is these relationships which are significant for conduct. It is these relationships alone which imply a unitary system of valuations.[1]

At one time it used to be thought that these

---

when the rich do support vast retinues of retainers, the retainers spend most of their time looking after each other. Anyone who has lived in a household in which there was more than one servant will realise the force of this consideration.

[1] On all this, the classical discussion is still to be found in Samuel Bailey's chapter (*op. cit.*, pp. 71-93) "On comparing commodities at different periods". Bailey overstates his case to this extent, that he does not mention *prospective* value relations through time (see below). But in every other respect his position is unassailable, and his demonstrations are among the most elegant to be found in the whole range of theoretical analysis. Even the most *blasé* could scarcely resist a thrill at the exquisite delicacy of his exhibition of the ambiguities of the first proposition of Ricardo's *Principles*. It was one of the few real injuries done to the progress of Economic Science by the solidarity of the English Classics that, presumably because of its attacks on Ricardo and Malthus, Bailey's work was allowed to drop into neglect. It is hardly an exaggeration to say that Index Number Theory is only today emancipating itself from errors into which a regard to Bailey's main proposition would effectively have prevented it from falling.

difficulties could be overcome by correcting individual prices for variations in the "value of money". And it may be admitted that, if the relations between each commodity and all the others save the one under consideration remained the same, and only the supply of money and the demand or supply of this particular commodity altered, such corrections would be sufficient. If, that is to say, the original price relationships were

$$P_a = P_b = P_c = P_d = P_e \ \ldots \ . \ (1)$$

and in the next period they were

$$P_a = \tfrac{1}{2}P_b = \tfrac{1}{2}P_c = \tfrac{1}{2}P_d = \tfrac{1}{2}P_e \ \ldots \ . \ (2)$$

then matters would be simple, and the comparison would have some meaning. But such a relationship is not possible save as a result of a series of compensatory accidents. This is not merely because demand or the conditions of production of *other commodities* may change. It is because any conceivable change, either real or monetary, must bring about *different* changes in the relation of a particular good to each other commodity. That is to say, save in the case of a compensatory accident, any change will lead not to a new set of relationships of the order of equation (2), but rather to a set of relationships of the order

$$P_a = \tfrac{1}{2}P_b = \tfrac{1}{4}P_c = \tfrac{3}{4}P_d = P_e \ \ldots \ . \ (3)$$

It has long been recognised that this must be the case with real changes. If the demand for *a* changes, it is most improbable that the demand for *b, c, d, e* . . . will change in such a way that the change in relation between *a* and *b* will be equivalent to the change in relation to *b* and *c* . . . and so on. With changes in technique, factors of production which are released from the production of a will not be likely to be distributed between b, c, d in such proportions as to preserve $P_b : P_c :: P_c : P_d$ . . . But, as has been demonstrated once and for all by Professor Hayek,[1] the same is true of "monetary" changes. It is almost impossible to conceive a "monetary" change which does not affect relative prices differently. But, if this is so, the idea of precise "correction" of price changes over time is illusory.[2] Samuel Bailey's conclusion remains: "When we say that an article in a former age was of a certain value, we mean that it exchanged for a certain quantity of some other commodity. But this is an inapplicable expression in speaking of only one commodity at two different periods."[3]

Here, again, it is important to realise the limitations of this proposition. It does not deny the possibility of intertemporal price relationships. Quite clearly, at any moment, anticipations of what prices will be at a future period inevitably influence present valuations and price relationships.[4] It is possible to exchange goods now for goods in the future, and we

---

[1] *Prices and Production*, especially ch. iii. See also Mises, *Theorie des Geldes und der Umlaufsmitteln*, pp. 358-375.

[2] It is not always realised that the difficulty of attaching precise meaning to the idea of changes in value, if there are more than two commodities and the ratios of exchange between one and the rest do not move in the same proportion, is not limited to the idea of changes in the "value of money". The problem of conceiving changes in the "purchasing power" of pig iron is just as insoluble as the problem of conceiving changes in the purchasing power of money. The difference is a practical one. The fact that production is determined by relative valuations makes it unnecessary for practical purposes to worry about changes in the purchasing power of pig iron, while for all sorts of reasons, some good, some bad, we are obliged to worry a good deal about the effects of "monetary" changes.

[3] *Op. cit.*, p. 72.

[4] See Fetter, *Economic Principles*, p. 101 *ff.*, and pp. 235-277. See also Hayek, *Das Intertemporale Gleichgewichtsystem der Preise und die Bewegungen des "Geldwertes"* (*Weltwirtschaftliches Archiv*, Bd. 28, pp. 33-76).

can conceive an equilibrium direction of price change through time. This is true and important. But while there is and must be a connection between present prices and anticipations of future prices, there is no necessary connection or significant value relationship between present prices and *past prices*. The conception of an equilibrium relationship through time is a hypothetical relationship. Through history, the given data change, and though *at every moment* there are tendencies towards an equilibrium, yet *from moment to moment* it is not the *same* equilibrium towards which there is movement. There is a fundamental asymmetry in price relationships through time. The future—the apparent future, that is to say—affects the present, but the past is irrelevant. The effects of the past are now simply part of the "given data". So far as value relationships are concerned, bygones are forever bygones.

Here, again, as in the case of our considerations regarding aggregates, there is no intention of denying the practical utility and significance of comparisons of certain prices over time, or of the value of "corrections" of these prices by suitably devised index numbers. It is not open to serious question that for certain questions of applied Economics on the one hand, and interpretation of history on the other, the index number technique is invaluable. Given a willingness to make arbitrary assumptions with regard to the significance of certain price sums, it is not denied that conclusions which are important for practice may be reached. All that it is desired to emphasise is that such conclusions do not follow from the categories of pure theory, and that they must necessarily involve a *conventional* element depending either upon the assumption of a certain empirical constancy of data[1] or upon arbitrary judgments of value with regard to the relative importance of particular prices.

6. The interpretation of economic statistics is not the only department of economic studies to be affected by this conception of our subject-matter. The arrangement and elaboration of the central body of theoretical analysis is also considerably modified. This is an interesting example of the utility of this kind of investigation. Starting from the intention to state more precisely the subject of our generalisations, we reach a point of view which enables us, not only to pick out what is essential and what is accidental in those generalisations, but also to restate them in such a way as to give their essential bearing much greater force. Let us see how this happens.

The traditional approach to Economics, at any rate among English-speaking economists, has been by way of an enquiry into the causes determining the production and distribution of wealth.[2] Economics has been divided into two main divisions, the Theory of Production and the Theory of Distribution, and the task of these theories has been to explain the causes

[1] As in discussions of changes in real income and the cost of living. On all this see Haberler, *Der Sinn der Indexzahlen, passim.* Dr. Haberler's conclusion is definitive. "Die Wissenschaft macht sich einer Grenzüberschreitung schuldig, sie fällt ein Werturteil wenn sie die Wirtschaftsubjekte belehren will welches von zwei Naturaleinkommen das 'grössere' Realeinkommen enthalt. Darüber zu entscheiden, welches vorzuziehen ist, sind einzig und allein die Wirtschafter selbst berufen" ("Science is guilty of trespassing beyond its necessary limits—that is to say, it is delivering a judgment of value—if it attempts to lay down for others which of two real incomes is the 'larger'. To decide on this, to decide which real income is to be preferred, is a task which can only be done by him who is to enjoy it— that is, by the individual as 'economic subject'". The translation is very free, for there is no English equivalent to the very useful German contrast between *Naturaleinkommen* and *Realeinkommen* unless we use "Real income" as equivalent to *Naturaleinkommen* and Fetter's "Psychic income" for the German *Realeinkommen*).

[2] See Cannan, *Theories of Production and Distribution,* ch. ii.

determining the size of the "total product" and the causes determining the proportions in which it is distributed between different factors of production and different persons. There have been minor differences of content under these two headings. There has always been a great deal of trouble about the position of the Theory of Value. But, speaking broadly, up to quite a recent date, this has been the main "cut" into the body of the subject.

Now, no doubt, there is a strong *prima facie* case for this procedure. As Professor Cannan urges,[1] the questions in which we are interested from the point of view of social policy are—or at any rate appear to be —questions relating to production and distribution. If we are contemplating the imposition of a tax or the granting of a subsidy, the questions we tend to ask (whether we understand what we mean or not) are: What will be the effects of this measure on production, What will be its effects on distribution? It is not unnatural, therefore, that, in the past, economists have tended to arrange their generalisations in the form of answers to these two questions.[2]

Yet, if we bear in mind what has been said already with regard to the nature of our subject-matter and the relativity of the "quantities" it contemplates, it should be fairly clear that from this

---

[1] "The fundamental questions of economics are why all of us taken together are as well off as we are and why some of us are much better off and others much worse off than the average . . ." (Cannan, *Wealth*, 3rd edition, p. v).

[2] Whether their generalisations *did* answer the questions, especially that relating to personal distribution, is another matter (see Cannan, *Economic Outlook*, pp. 215-253, and *Review of Economic Theory*, pp. 284-332; see also Dalton, *Inequality of Incomes*, pp. 33-158). The point is that they thought they ought to answer them. The fact that they did not is not necessarily to the discredit either of economists or their generalisations. There is strong reason for supposing that personal distribution is determined in part by extra-economic causes.

point of view the traditional division has serious deficiencies.

It should not be necessary at this stage to dwell upon the inappropriateness of the various technical elements which almost inevitably intrude into a system arranged on this principle. We have all felt, with Professor Schumpeter, a sense almost of shame at the incredible banalities of much of the so-called theory of production—the tedious discussions of the various forms of peasant proprietorship, factory organisation, industrial psychology, technical education, etc., which are apt to occur in even the best treatises on general theory arranged on this plan.[1] One has only to compare the masterly sweep of Book V. of Marshall's *Principles*, which deals with problems which are strictly economic in our sense, with the spineless platitudes about manures[2] and the "fine natures among domestic servants"[3] of much of Book IV. to realise the insidious effect of a procedure which opens the door to the intrusions of amateur technology into discussions which should be purely economic.

But there is a more fundamental objection to this procedure; it necessarily precludes precision. Scientific generalisations, if they are to pretend to the status of laws, must be capable of being stated exactly. That does not mean, as we shall see in a later chapter, that they must be capable of quantitative exactitude. We do not need to give numerical values to the law of demand to be in a position to use it for deducing important consequences. But we do need to state it

---

[1] See Schumpeter, *Das Wesen und der Hauptinhalt der theoretischen Nationalökonomie*, p. 156.

[2] *Principles*, 8th edition, pp. 145-146.

[3] *Ibid.*, p. 207.

in such a way as to make it relate to formal relations which are capable of being *conceived* exactly.[1]

Now, as we have seen already, the idea of changes in the total volume of production has no precise content. We may, if we please, attach certain conventional values to certain indices and say that we *define* a change in production as a change in this index; for certain purposes this may be advisable. But there is no analytical justification for this procedure. It does not follow from our conception of an economic good. The kind of empirical generalisation which may be made concerning what causes will affect production in this sense, can never achieve the status of a law. For a law must relate to definite conceptions and relationships; and a change in the aggregate of production is not a definite conception.

As a matter of fact, nothing which can really be called a "law" of production in this sense has ever been elaborated.[2] Whenever the generalisations of economists have assumed the form of laws, they have related not to vague notions such as the total product, but to perfectly definite concepts such as price, supply, demand, and so on. The Ricardian System which, in

---

[1] See Edgeworth, *Mathematical Psychics*, pp. 1-6; Kaufmann, *Was kann die mathematische Methode in der Nationalökonomie leisten?* (*Zeitschrift für Nationalökonomie*, Bd. 2, pp. 754-779).

[2] The nearest approach to a law of production is embodied in the celebrated Optimum Theory of Population. This starts from the perfectly precise law of Non-proportional Returns which relates to variations of productivity in the proportionate combinations of individual factors, and *appears* to achieve a similar precision in regard to variations of all human factors in a fixed material environment. In fact, however, it introduces conceptions of averages and aggregates to which it is impossible to give meaning without conventional assumptions. On the Optimum Theory see my *Optimum Theory of Population* in *London Essays in Economics*, edited by Dalton and Gregory. In that essay I discussed the difficulties of averaging, but I had not then perceived the full weight of the general methodological difference between statements relating to averages and statements relating to precise quantities. Hence my emphasis on this point is insufficient.

this respect, provides the archetype of all subsequent systems, is essentially a discussion of the tendencies to equilibrium of clear-cut quantities and relationships. It is no accident that wherever its discussions have related to separate types of economic goods and ratios of exchange between economic goods, there the generalisations of Economics have assumed the form of scientific laws.[1]

For this reason, in recent years Economists have tended more and more to abandon the traditional arrangement. We no longer enquire concerning the causes determining variations of production and distribution. We enquire rather concerning the conditions of equilibrium of various economic "quantities",[2] given certain initial data, and we enquire concerning the effects of variations of these data. Instead of dividing our central body of analysis into a Theory of Production and a Theory of Distribution, we have a Theory of Equilibrium and a Theory of Variations.[3] Instead of regarding the economic system as a gigantic machine for turning out an aggregate product and proceeding to enquire what causes make this product greater or less, and in what proportions this product

---

[1] It is important not to overstress the excellence of past procedure. The theory of money, *e.g.*, although in many respects the most highly developed branch of Economic Theory, has continually employed pseudo-concepts of the sort we have just declared suspect—the price level, movements of purchasing power parities, etc. But it is just here that the difficulties of monetary theory have persisted. And recent improvements in monetary theory have been directed to eliminating all dependence on these fictions.

[2] On the various types of equilibrium contemplated, see Knight, *Risk, Uncertainty and Profit*, p. 143, note; Wicksell, *Vorlesungen über National-ökonomie*, Bd. 1; and Robbins, *On a Certain Ambiguity in the Conception of Stationary Equilibrium* (*Economic Journal*, vol. xl., pp. 194-214).

[3] If I am not mistaken, the title Theory of Variations was first used in this context by Professor Schumpeter, *op cit.*, p. 441 *seq.* The content of the theory is, of course, older than Ricardo.

is divided, we regard it as a series of interdependent but conceptually discrete relationships between men and economic goods; and we ask under what conditions these relationships are constant and what are the effects of changes in either the ends or the means between which they mediate.

As we have seen already, this tendency, although in its completest form very modern indeed, has its origin very early in the literature of scientific Economics. Quesnay's *Tableau Economique* was essentially an attempt to apply what is now called equilibrium analysis. And, although Adam Smith's great work professed to deal with the causes of the wealth of nations, and did in fact make many remarks on the general question of the conditions of opulence which are of great importance in any history of Applied Economics, yet, from the point of view of the history of Theoretical Economics, the central achievement of his book was his demonstration of the mode in which the division of labour tended to be kept in equilibrium by the mechanism of relative prices—a demonstration which, as Allyn Young has shown,[1] is in harmony with the most refined apparatus of the modern School of Lausanne. The theory of Value and Distribution was really the central core of the analysis of the Classics, try as they might to conceal their objects under other names. And the traditional theory relating to the effects of taxes and bounties was always couched in terms thoroughly consistent with the procedure of the modern Theory of Variations. Thus, though the appearance of modern theory may be new, its substance is continuous with what was most essential in the old. The modern arrangement simply

[1] *Op cit.*, pp. 540-542.

makes explicit the methodological foundations of the earlier theories and generalises the procedure.[1]

At first sight it might be thought that these innovations ran the risk of over-austerity; that they involved dispensing with a mass of theory which is genuinely illuminating. Such a belief would be founded on an absence of knowledge of the potentialities of the new procedure. It may safely be asserted that there is nothing which fits into the old framework, which cannot be more satisfactorily exhibited in the new. The only difference is that, at every step in the new arrangement, we know exactly the limitations and implications of our knowledge. If we step outside the sphere of pure analysis and adopt any of the conventional assumptions of Applied Economics, we know just where we are. We are never in danger of asserting as an implication of our fundamental premises something which is smuggled in on the way by means of a conventional assumption.

We may take as an example of the advantages of this procedure the modern treatment of organisation of production. The old treatment of this subject was hopelessly unsatisfactory: A few trite generalisations about the advantages of the division of labour copied from Adam Smith, and illustrated perhaps by a few examples from Babbage; then extensive discursions

[1] The beginning of the change dates from the coming of the Subjective Theory of Value. So long as the Theory of Value was expounded in terms of costs, it was possible to regard the subject-matter of Economics as something social and collective, and to discuss price relationships simply as market phenomena. With the realisation that these market phenomena were, in fact, dependent on the interplay of individual choice, and that the very social phenomena in terms of which they were explained—costs—were in the last analysis the reflex of individual choice—the valuation of alternative opportunities (Wieser, Davenport)—this approach becomes less and less convenient. The work of the mathematical economists in this respect only sets out particularly boldly a procedure which is really common to all modern theory.

on industrial "forms" and the "entrepreneur" with
a series of thoroughly unscientific and question-begging
remarks on national characteristics—the whole wound
up, perhaps, with a chapter on localisation. There is
no need to dwell on the insufferable dreariness and
mediocrity of all this. But it is perhaps just as well
to state definitely its glaring positive deficiencies. It
suggests that from the point of view of the economist
"organisation" is a matter of internal industrial (or
agricultural) arrangement—if not internal to the firm,
at any rate internal to "the" industry. At the same
time it tends to leave out completely the governing
factor of all productive organisation—the relationship
of prices and costs. That comes in a different division
which deals with "value". As a result, as almost any
teacher who has taken over students reared on the
old textbooks will realise, it was quite possible for a
man to have an extensive knowledge of value theory
and its copious refinements and to be able to prattle
away at great length about the rate of interest and its
possible "causes", without ever having realised the
fundamental part played by prices, costs, and interest
rates in the organisation of production.

In the modern treatment this is impossible. In the
modern treatment, discussion of "production" is an
integral part of the Theory of Equilibrium. It is shown
how factors of production are distributed between the
production of different goods by the mechanism of
prices and costs, how given certain fundamental data,
interest rates, and price margins determine the distribution of factors between production for the present
and production for the future. The doctrine of division
of labour, heretofore so disagreeably technological,
becomes an integral feature of a theory of moving

equilibrium through time.[1] Even the question of "internal" organisation and administration now becomes related to an outside network of relative prices and costs; and since this is how things work in practice, what is at first sight the greater remoteness of pure theory in fact brings us much nearer to reality.

[1] The best discussions are to be found in Wicksell, *Vorlesungen*, Bd. 1, pp. 158-290; Hans Mayer, *Produktion in the Handwörterbuch der Staatswissenschaft.*

CHAPTER IV

THE NATURE OF ECONOMIC GENERALISATIONS

1. WE have now sufficiently discussed the subject-matter of Economics and the fundamental conceptions associated therewith. But we have not yet discussed the nature of the generalisations whereby these conceptions are related. We have not yet discussed the nature and derivation of Economic Laws. This, therefore, is the purpose of the present chapter. When it is completed we shall be in a position to proceed to our second main task—investigation of the limitations and significance of this system of generalisations.

2. It is the object of this Essay to arrive at conclusions which are based on the inspection of Economic Science as it actually exists. Its aim is not to discover how Economics should be pursued—that controversy, although we shall have occasion to refer to it *en passant*,[1] may be regarded as settled as between reasonable people—but rather what significance is to be attached to the results which it has already achieved. It will be convenient, therefore, at the outset of our investigations, if, instead of attempting to derive the nature of Economic Generalisations from the pure categories of our subject-

[1] See below, Chapter V., Section 3.

matter,[1] we commence by examining a typical specimen.

It is a well-known generalisation of elementary Price Theory that, in a free market, intervention by some outside body to fix a price below the market price will lead to an excess of demand over supply. This proposition, although usually ignored by statesmen and writers in the popular press, has been demonstrated so often in practice that, even from the point of view of "straightforward common sense" (*i.e.*, naïve acceptance of the apparent evidence of experience) there can be little doubt concerning its validity.[2] Upon what foundations does it rest?

It should not be necessary to spend much time showing that it cannot rest upon any appeal to History. The frequent concomitance of certain phenomena in time may suggest a problem to be solved. It cannot by itself be taken to imply a definite causal relationship. It might be shown that, whenever the fixing of maximum prices in relatively free markets has taken place, it has been followed, either by evasion or by the kind of distributive chaos which we associate with the food queues of the late War or the French Revolution. But this would not prove that the two phenomena were causally connected in any intimate sense. Nor would it afford any safe ground for prediction with regard to their future relationship. In the

---

[1] For an example of such a derivation reaching substantially similar results, see Strigl, *op. cit.*, p. 121 *seq.*

[2] If any reader of this book has any doubt of the evidence of the facts, he should consult the standard work on recent British experiments in such measures, *British Food Control*, by Sir William Beveridge. It is worth noting that unanimity among experts has not prevented the introduction of a Profiteering Act during the present crisis (21 and 22 Geo. V., cap. 51), although it may be suspected that expert knowledge in the departments which might have administered it, has prevented it becoming anything but a dead letter.

absence of rational grounds for supposing intimate connection, there would be no sufficient reason for supposing that History "would repeat itself". For if there is one thing which *is* shown by History, not less than by elementary logic, it is that historical induction, unaided by the analytical judgment, is the worst possible basis of prophecy.[1] "History shows", commences the bore at the club, and we resign ourselves to the prediction of the improbable. It is one of the great merits of the modern Philosophy of History that it has repudiated all claims of this sort, and indeed makes it the *fundamentum divisionis* between History and Natural Science that history does not proceed by way of generalising abstraction.[2]

It is equally clear that our belief does not rest upon the results of controlled experiment. It is perfectly true that this particular proposition has on more than one occasion been exemplified by the results of government intervention carried out under conditions which might be held to bear some resemblance to the conditions of controlled experiment. But it would be gross superficiality to suppose that the results of these experiments can be held to justify a proposition of such universality as the proposition we are examining. Certainly it would be a very fragile body of Economic Generalisations which could be erected on a basis of this sort. Yet, in fact, our belief in this particular

---

[1] "The vulgar notion that the safe methods on political subjects are those of Baconian induction—that the true guide is not general reasoning but specific experience—will one day be quoted as among the most unequivocal marks of a low state of the speculative faculties of any age in which it is accredited. . . . Whoever makes use of an argument of this kind . . . should be sent back to learn the elements of some one of the more easy physical sciences. Such reasoners ignore the fact of Plurality of Causes in the very case which affords the most signal example of it" (John Stuart Mill, *Logic*, chapter x., paragraph 8).

[2] See Rickert, *op. cit.*, pp. 78-101, *Die Grenzen der Naturwissenschaftlichen Begriffsbildung, passim.* See also Max Weber, *op. cit., passim.*

generalisation and many others is more complete than belief based upon any number of controlled experiments.

But on what, then, does it depend?

Let us look more closely at the arguments by which it is established. The proposition that a price fixed below the equilibrium point must result in an excess of demand over supply is a simple corollary of the general Theory of Price. According to that theory, the equilibrium price must be conceived as that price which restricts demand to the available supply. It follows quite simply that if the price is lower than this, the necessary restriction will not be effected. Demand which would have been excluded by the higher price will arise and there will be disequilibrium.

But why should we assume that there exist demands which must be excluded at a price at which demand and supply are equal? Surely this follows from the fact that a price exists at all. If there were no demand beyond the available supply, and no alternative use for the factors of production involved,[1] there would be no price. The good would not be scarce in relation to the demand for it. It would not be an economic good at all. It would be a free good.

In the last analysis, therefore, our proposition rests upon deductions which are implicit in our initial definition of the subject-matter of Economic Science as a whole. Economics is concerned with the disposal of scarce goods with alternative uses. That is our fundamental conception. And from this conception

[1] The qualifying clause is necessary to take account of the case where, although the demand curve becomes parallel to the y axis, the transferability of the cost factors keeps the supply within the limits of active demand. This case is covered explicitly by the generalisation of paragraph 3. Where goods are reproducible, the scarcity of the factors is fundamental.

we are enabled to derive the whole complicated structure of modern Price Theory. That goods are scarce and have alternative uses is a fact. Economic analysis consists in elucidating the manifold implications thereof.

The same thing can be put in a form which, although apparently more pretentious, may perhaps carry more conviction to those who are accustomed to the jargon of modern theory. The proposition that the fixing of a price below the equilibrium price necessarily results in an excess of demand over supply, involves the assumption of a demand schedule that increases as price diminishes—in the language of co-ordinate geometry, a downward sloping demand curve. But, as is well known, this assumption in turn involves the assumption of individual scales of relative valuation which show diminishing marginal significance as supply is assumed to increase. But this, too, is implicit in the conception of goods which are scarce in relation to the use which might be made of them. The assumption that some specific uses, either of the good itself or of the factors which produce it, must be relinquished so long as the good remains an economic good implies just that hierarchy of uses which underlies the various applications of the Law of Diminishing Marginal Utility.[1]

3. The example we have just examined was natur-

[1] On the concept of scales of the relative marginal significance of various commodities, see especially Wicksteed, *Commonsense of Political Economy*, pp. 1-125; Rosenstein-Rodan, art. *Grenznutzen* in the *Handwörterbuch der Staatswissenschaft*, Bd. 4, pp. 1190-1223. (This article, in addition to being itself no mean addition to the literature of marginal utility theory, contains a very valuable bibliography of that literature.)   Viner, *The Utility Concept in Value Theory and its Critics* (*Journal of Political Economy*, vol. xxxiii., pp. 369-387); and Knight, *Risk, Uncertainty and Profit*, pp. 51-93. It should be noted that the scales are individual scales. They involve no assumption of a superpersonal collective utility. See below, Chapter VI., Section 2.

ally of the simplest order. But nevertheless it is typical of the whole range of analytical Economics. From the fundamental concept of goods which are scarce in relation to the demand for them we derive the idea of scales or functions expressing the relative valuation put upon these goods by different individuals. We then make various suppositions concerning the technical and legal conditions under which production and exchange may be assumed to be possible, and we examine, on the one hand, what are the conditions of equilibrium in these various circumstances, and, on the other, what are the implications of changes in the given data. On the analytical side Economics proves to be a series of deductions from the fundamental concept of scarcity of time and materials.

It is worth while spending a little longer examining the grounds for this verdict, for it is not always realised how far the theoretical developments of the last half century have succeeded in unifying analytical economics on the lines we have indicated; and at first sight the position may appear paradoxical. Analytical Economics did not originate consciously in this manner. It arose from attempts to provide practical answers to very practical questions. It was only after a long process of development that it became possible to detect in the various solutions the common element we have isolated. And even at the present day, the formulation of general theory is often marred by a quite unnecessary eclecticism. Unless it is made quite clear that in the marginal analysis we possess the basis for a completely unitary Economic Theory, it is safe to say that the inner significance of that analysis has not been recognised at all.

A good example of what we have to elucidate is to be found in the Law of Costs. Under competitive conditions in equilibrium the price of commodities is equal to their cost of production per unit—cost of production of course being taken to include what Marshall called expenses of management. How does this follow from the fundamental concept we have elaborated?

Until quite recently the connection was not understood. In the classical system, cost of production, in the sense of the "real" counterpart of money expenses, tended to be exhibited as something ultimate. For purposes of analysis, commodities were separated into two groups, commodities whose value was determined by their scarcity, and commodities whose value was determined by their cost of production either in the sense of labour cost or labour plus abstinence.[1] In the one case the play of demand was regarded as the determining factor; in the other, cost of production in one or other of the senses just mentioned. And even in modern times the psychological forces working on the supply side have been thought to be something entirely different from the forces working on the demand side. Marginal utility and cost of production—

---

[1] See, e.g., Ricardo, *Principles* (ed. McCulloch), p. 9. It is not true, as certain critics of the classics have alleged, that the best classics regarded supply and demand and cost of production as distinct principles of explanation. In the *Notes on Malthus*, Ricardo makes it quite clear that he understood cost of production as an influence limiting supply. ("Mr. Malthus mistakes the question—I do not say that the value of a commodity will always conform to its natural price without an additional supply, but I say that the cost of production regulates the supply and therefore regulates the price" [p. 21]). Francis Horner in his review of Canard's *Principes d'Economie Politique* in the *Edinburgh Review*, vol. ii., 1803, pp. 437-450, puts the matter as well as it has been put by any modern: "The proper mode of introducing this principle" (*i.e.*, the cost principle) "into the theory of exchangeable value, is, not to state the value of labour as constituting the whole price or forming the adequate measure of it, but to view it as a condition which limits the eventual supply of each commodity" (*ibid.*, p. 437).

these were the two blades of Marshall's celebrated pair of scissors.

It is one of the great achievements of Wieser and his successors that this duality has been removed.[1] The expenses of producing a given commodity fall into two types of outlay—outlays on factors of production which are specialised to produce the goods in question and no others (specific factors), and outlays on factors which are not so specialised (non-specific factors). Now, so far as the outlays due to the specific factors are concerned, it is fairly clear that the scarcity of these factors, and hence their price, is derived from the scarcity of the product. No independent principle of explanation is needed here. But so far as the outlays for the non-specific factors are concerned, at first sight the price is something given independently of the conditions of demand. And of course it is perfectly true that it may be considered as being to some extent independent of the conditions of demand for the particular product under consideration. But just as it is illegitimate to consider the valuations of one good independently of the valuation of other goods, so it is illegitimate to regard the valuation of the services of productive factors as exhausting itself *via* the demand in any one line of production. Once this is realised the rest is simple. What is it which causes the price paid for a given factor of production in a given

---

[1] *Ursprung und Hauptgesetze des Wirtschaftlichen Werthes*, pp. 146-170; *Natural Value*, pp. 171-214. See also the juvenile work, *Über das Verhältnis der Kosten zum Wert*, printed in the *Gesammelte Abhandlungen*, pp. 377-404. On the significance of Wieser's achievement in this field see Mayer, *Friedrich Wieser zum Gedächtnis, Zeitschrift für Volkswirtschaft und Sozialpolitik, N.F.,* Bd. 5, p. 636. Wicksteed's *Commonsense of Political Economy* contains an extensive statement of the modern law of cost in general Equilibrium Theory. Dr. Haberler's *Die Theorie des Komparativen Kosten* (*Weltwirtschaftliches Archiv*, Bd. 31, p. 349) contains an extension of this law to the special case of international equilibrium.

80 SIGNIFICANCE OF ECONOMIC SCIENCE CH.

line of production to be what it is and not something
else? Clearly the demand in that line of production in
relation to the supply. But why is the supply of the
factors in that line limited to what it is? Why is not
the whole supply devoted to this line of production?
Clearly because there is demand for the scarce products which it can produce *elsewhere*. Its price in one
line therefore depends upon the price which is put
upon it in others. In the end, subjective valuations
govern costs equally with product prices.

It has sometimes been objected that this unification is only possible on the assumption that the total
supplies of factors of production are constant. Given
flexible supply, it is urged that the concept of real
cost once more comes into its own as an independent
principle of explanation. In the nineties this view
was strongly supported by Edgeworth.[1] At the present
day its most distinguished exponent is Mr. D. H.
Robertson.[2]

The objection is plausible. And it may be admitted
that, as against the form in which the arguments of the
early Austrians were cast, it has a certain degree of
validity. It is clear that, for expository purposes, both
Wieser and Böhm-Bawerk had recourse to the hypothesis of fixed total factor-supplies, while their opponents, Marshall and Edgeworth, always proceeded
from the assumption that factor-supplies were flexible.[3]

[1] Böhm-Bawerk on the Ultimate Standard of Value, *Papers relating to
Political Economy*, vol. iii., pp. 59-64.
[2] See, *e.g.*, *Economic Fragments*, p. 21. Mr. Robertson's explicit pro-
nouncements on this subject are tantalisingly concise. But I am sure he
would not regard it as unfair to say that reliance on the real cost concept
informs much of his most characteristic work.
[3] For a fuller elucidation of the difference of assumption involved, see
my *On a Certain Ambiguity in the Conception of Stationary Equilibrium*
(*Economic Journal*, vol. xl., pp. 194-214). See also my *Economic Works of
Philip Wicksteed* (*Economica*, December, 1930, pp. 253-256).

But even if we proceed from the wider hypothesis Wieser's proposition still holds. The total supply of work depends upon the relative valuation of the product of work and leisure. The supply of capital depends upon the relative valuation of income now and income in the future. The intricate interrelationships of the Stationary State all resolve themselves into what Pareto called an equilibrium of tastes and obstacles. On the one side we have scales of relative valuation: on the other the given facts of the technique of production and the material and human equipment.[1]

Again, we may take the theory of money. Money is a commodity whose absolute quantity in static conditions has no significance for the behaviour of any member of the community. For many years, therefore, it was thought that the fundamental principles of the Theory of Money were different in kind from the principles involved in non-monetary analysis. The value of money was explained in terms radically different from the terms involved in the general theory of value. The total quantity of money was opposed to the total quantity of goods and services exchanged against it; and its value per unit in any given period was held to be determined by the quantity multiplied by the velocity of circulation divided by the volume of trade—the celebrated equation of exchange $\dfrac{MV}{T} = P$.

---

[1] It is easy to see that in carrying through the more elaborate forms of analysis recourse may very often be conveniently made to the language of mathematics. No logical difference exists between theory which employs symbols and theory which is content with words. The choice is solely a matter of convenience. See Kaufmann, *Was kann die mathematische Methode in Nationalökonomie leisten?* (*Zeitschrift für Nationalökonomie*, Bd. 2, pp. 754-779).

From a purely formal point of view no doubt this procedure was valid. MV must equal PT because they are just the same quantities set out in a different manner.[1] It is a mere tautology, though no doubt it is significant in the discussion of certain problems. Certainly the old quantity theory of money has a practical utility whose value should not be underrated.

But there is nothing in the equation of exchange which *explains* the ratio of exchange between the unit of account and other things in the circle of exchange. Nor is there anything which relates it to individual conduct. *Prima facie* it is not based upon any general principle deduced from the fundamental categories of pure theory.

Again modern analysis has effected the desired unification. Working on the basis of the general Law of Diminishing Marginal Significance, Marshall[2] and Cannan[3] in this country, and Mises[4] in Austria, have succeeded in showing how individual demand for money may be formulated in terms strictly symmetrical with the conception of demand for other things, so that ultimately the value of money, equally with the value of anything else, may be explained in terms of relative subjective valuations. For the community as a whole, the quantity of money may be a matter of indifference. But, for the individual with given resources, to keep a certain proportion of these resources available in the form of free cash is in itself a convenience. Hence there arises a demand for money

---

[1] See Marshall, *Money, Credit and Commerce*, p. 48; Haberler, *Kritische Bemerkungen zur Schumpeter Geldtheorie* (*Zeitschrift für Volkswirtschaft und Sozialpolitik N.F.*, vol. iv., 1925, pp. 647-668).

[2] *Official Papers*, pp. 43-45.

[3] *Money* (4th edition), pp. 10-17 and 71-79.

[4] *Theorie des Geldes*, pp. 85-146.

to hold—a relative valuation of cash and other resources which is expressed "in" the system of relative prices equally with other valuations. It is characteristic of this synthesis, as of many others, that while achieving much greater logical and æsthetic elegance than the old theory, it yet retains all that was useful and valid in it. It is not necessary here to show how the old conception of velocity of circulation can be derived from the modern conception of demand for money: the thing has been done very frequently.[1] All that it has been desired to indicate is the fundamental unity of economic analysis. Not only the general Theory of Economic Equilibrium, but also the pure Theory of Money, can be deduced from the fundamental conception of goods which are scarce in relation to the possible uses which may be made of them.

4. If this is true, economic analysis turns out to be, as Fetter has emphasised,[2] the elucidation of the implications of the necessity of choice in various assumed circumstances. In pure Mechanics we explore the implication of the existence of certain given properties of bodies. In pure Economics we examine the implication of the existence of scarce means with alternative uses. The assumption of scales of relative valuation is the foundation of all subsequent complications.

It is sometimes thought, even at the present day, that this notion of scales of relative valuation depends upon the validity of particular psychological doctrines. The borderlands of Economics are the happy hunting-ground of the charlatan and the quack, and, in these

---

[1] See, e.g., Pigou, *Essays in Applied Economics*, pp. 174-178.
[2] *Economic Principles*, pp. ix and 12-21.

ambiguous regions, in recent years, endless time has been devoted to the acquisition of cheap notoriety by attacks on the alleged psychological assumptions of Economic Science. Psychology, it is said, advances very rapidly. If, therefore, Economics rests upon particular psychological doctrines, there is no task more ready to hand for the intellectually sterile, than every five years or so to write sharp polemics showing that, since psychology has changed its fashion, Economics needs "rewriting from the foundations upwards". As might be expected, the opportunity has not been neglected. Professional economists, absorbed in the exciting task of discovering new truth, have usually disdained to reply: and the lay public, ever anxious to escape the necessity of recognising the implications of choice in a world of scarcity, has allowed itself to be bamboozled into believing that matters, which are in fact as little dependent on the truth of fashionable psychology as the multiplication table, are still open questions on which the enlightened man, who, of course, is nothing if not a psychologist, must be willing to suspend judgment.

Unfortunately, in the past, incautious utterances on the part of economists themselves have sometimes afforded a pretext for these strictures. It is well known that certain of the founders of the modern Subjective Theory of Value did in fact claim the authority of the doctrines of psychological hedonism as sanctions for their propositions. This was not true of the Austrians. From the beginning the Mengerian tables were constructed in terms which begged no psychological questions.[1] Böhm-Bawerk explicitly repudiated any affiliation with psychological hedonism; indeed,

[1] See Menger, *Grundsätze*, pp. 77-152.

he went to infinite pains to avoid this kind of misconception.[1] But the names of Gossen and Jevons and Edgeworth, to say nothing of their English followers, are a sufficient reminder of a line of really competent economists who did make pretensions of this sort. Gossen's *Entwicklung der Gesetze des menschlichen Verkehrs* certainly invokes hedonistic postulates. Jevons in his *Theory of Political Economy* prefaces his Theory of Utility and Exchange with a theory of pleasure and pain. Edgeworth commences his *Mathematical Psychics* with a section which urges the conception of "man as a pleasure machine".[2] Attempts have even been made to exhibit the Law of Diminishing Marginal Utility as a special case of the Weber-Fechner Law.[3]

But it is fundamentally important to distinguish between the actual practice of economists, and the logic which it implies, and their occasional *ex post facto* apologia. It is just this distinction which the critics of Economic Science fail to make. They inspect with supererogatory zeal the external façade, but they shrink from the intellectual labour of examining the inner structure. Nor do they trouble to acquaint themselves with the more modern formulations of the theory they are attacking. No doubt this has strategic advantages, for, in polemics of this kind, honest misconception is an excellent spur to effective rhetoric; and no one who was acquainted with modern value theory could honestly continue to argue that it has any essential connection with psychological hedonism,

[1] See *Positive Theorie des Kapitals*, 4ᵉ Auflage, pp. 232-246.

[2] *Mathematical Psychics*, p. 15.

[3] For a conclusive refutation of this view, which, however, itself rests upon a certain degree of misconception of the logical basis of Economic Analysis, see Max Weber, *Die Grenznutzlehre und das psychophysische Grundgesetz* (*Archiv für Sozialwissenschaft und Sozialpolitik*, vol. xxix., 1909).

or for that matter with any other brand of *Fach-Psychologie*. If the psychological critics of Economics had troubled to do these things they would speedily have perceived that the hedonistic trimmings of the works of Jevons and his followers were incidental to the main structure of a theory which—as the parallel development in Vienna showed—is capable of being set out and defended in absolutely non-hedonistic terms. As we have seen already, all that is assumed in the idea of the scales of valuation is that different goods have different uses and that these different uses have different significances for action, such that in a given situation one use will be preferred before another and one good before another. Why the human animal attaches particular values in this behaviouristic sense to particular things, is a question which we do not discuss. That may be quite properly a question for psychologists or perhaps even physiologists. All that we need to assume is the obvious fact that different possibilities offer different stimuli to behaviour, and that these stimuli can be arranged in order of their intensity.[1] The various theorems which may be derived from this fundamental conception are capable of explaining a manifold of social activity more varied and rich in its substance than anything yet entering the psychological laboratory. But they do this, not by assuming some particular psychology, but by regarding the things which psychology studies as the given data of their own deductions. Here, as so often, the founders of Economic Science constructed something more universal in its application than anything that they themselves claimed.

---

[1] That this does not assume the possibility of measuring valuations has been already sufficiently emphasised in Chapter III., Section 4, above.

5. But if this is so, what are we to say of the oft-reiterated accusation that Economics assumes a world of economic men concerned only with money-making and self-interest? Foolish and exasperating as this may appear to any competent economist, it is worth some further examination. Although it is completely false, yet there is a certain expository device of pure analysis which, if not explained in detail, might give rise to structures of this nature.

The general absurdity of the belief that the world contemplated by the economist is peopled only by egotists or "pleasure machines" should be sufficiently clear from what has been said already. The fundamental concept of economic analysis is the idea of scales of relative valuations; and, as we have seen, while we assume that different goods have different values at different margins, we do not regard it as part of our problem to explain why these particular valuations exist. We take them as given data. So far as we are concerned, our economic subjects can be pure egoists, pure altruists, pure ascetics, pure sensualists or—what is much more likely—mixed bundles of all these impulses. The scales of relative valuation are merely a convenient formal way of exhibiting certain permanent characteristics of man as he actually is. Failure to recognise the primacy of these valuations is simply a failure to understand the significance of the last sixty years of Economic Science.

Now the valuations which determine particular transactions may be of various degrees of complexity. In my purchase of bread I may be interested solely in the comparison between the bread and the other things in the circle of exchange on which I might have spent the money. But I may be interested too in the

happiness of my baker. There may exist between us
certain liens which make it preferable for me to buy
bread from him, rather than procure it from his com-
petitor who is willing to sell it a little cheaper. In
exactly the same way, in my sale of my own labour or
the hire of my property, I may be interested only in
the things which I receive as a result of the transaction; or I may be interested also in the experience of
labouring in one way rather than another, or in the
prestige or discredit, the feeling of virtue or shame in
hiring out my property in this line rather than in that.

All these things are taken into account in our conception of scales of relative valuation. And the
generalisations descriptive of economic equilibrium
are couched in a form which explicitly brings this to
the fore. Every first-year student since the days of
Adam Smith has learnt to describe equilibrium in the
distribution of particular grades of labour in terms of
a tendency, *not* to the maximisation of *money gains*,
but to the maximisation of *net advantages* in the
various alternatives open.[1] The modern theory of risk,
too, and its influence on the capital market depends
essentially on assumptions of this kind.[2] But sometimes for purposes of exposition it is convenient to
start from the first approximation that the valuation
is simple, and that, on the one side is a simple thing
desired or offered, and on the other is the money to be

---

[1] See Cantillon, *Essai sur la Nature du Commerce* (Higgs' edition), p. 21;
Adam Smith, *Wealth of Nations*, Bk. I., ch. x; Senior, *Political Economy*,
pp. 200-216; McCulloch, *Political Economy*, pp. 364-378; J. S. Mill, *Political
Economy*, 5th edition, vol. i., pp. 460-483; Marshall, *Principles*, 8th edition,
pp. 546-558—to take a representative sample of what would be regarded as
the more hard-boiled English tradition. For an up-to-date version of these
doctrines, see Wicksteed, *Commonsense of Political Economy*, Part I., *passim*.

[2] See Knight, *Risk, Uncertainty and Profit*, Part III.; Hicks, *The Theory
of Profit* (*Economica*, No. 31, pp. 170-190).

got or given in exchange for it. For the elucidation of certain complicated propositions such as the Theory of Imputation or marginal productivity analysis it permits an economy of terms. It is not in the least difficult, at the appropriate stage, to remove these assumptions and to pass to analysis couched in terms of complete formal generality.

This, then, is all that lies behind the occasional appearance of the *homo œconomicus*—the purely formal assumption that in certain exchange relationships all the means, so to speak, are on one side and all the ends on the other. If, *e.g.*, for purposes of demonstrating the circumstances in which a single price will emerge in a limited market, it is assumed that in my dealings in that market I always buy from the cheapest seller, it is not assumed at all that I am necessarily actuated by egotistical motives. On the contrary, it is well known that the impersonal relationship postulated is to be seen in its purest form when trustees, not being in a position to allow themselves the luxury of more complicated relationships, are trying to make the best terms for the estates they administer. All that it means is that my relation to the dealers does not enter into my hierarchy of ends. For me (who may be acting for myself or my friends or some civic or charitable authority) they are regarded merely as means. Or, again, if it is assumed—which in fact is usually done for purposes of showing *by contrast* what the total influences in equilibrium bring about—that I sell my labour always in the dearest market, it is not assumed that money and self-interest are my ultimate objects—I may be working entirely to support some philanthropic institution. It is assumed only that, so far as that transaction is concerned, my labour is only a means to an end; it is not to be regarded as an end in itself.

If this were commonly known, if it were generally realised that Economic Man is only an expository device—a first approximation used very cautiously at one stage in the development of arguments which, in their full development, neither employ any such assumption nor demand it in any way for a justification of their procedure—it is improbable that he would be such a universal bogey. But of course it is generally thought that he has a wider significance, that he lurks behind all those generalisations of the "Laws of Supply and Demand" better described as the Theory of Variations, whose elucidation so often is inimical to the universal desire to be able to believe it to be possible both to have your cake and to eat it. And it is for this reason that he is so furiously attacked. If it were Economic Man who barred the gates of Cloud-cuckoo-land, then it might well seem that a little psychology —it does not matter much of what brand—might be expected to burst them open.

Unfortunately this belief rests upon complete misapprehension. The propositions of the Theory of Variations do not in the least involve the assumption that men are actuated *only* by considerations of money gains and losses. They involve only the assumption that money plays *some* part in the valuation of the given alternatives. And they suggest only that if from any position of equilibrium the money incentive is *varied* this must tend to alter the equilibrium valuations. Money may not be regarded as playing a predominant part in the situation contemplated. So long as it plays some part then the propositions are applicable.

A simple illustration should make this quite plain. Let us suppose that a small bounty is granted in respect of the production of an article produced under conditions of free competition. According to the Theory of Variations there will be a tendency for the production of that commodity to increase—the magnitude of the increase depending upon considerations of elasticity into which it is not necessary for us to enter. Now upon what does this generalisation depend? Upon the assumption that producers are actuated only by considerations of monetary gain? Not at all. We may assume that they take into account all the "other advantages and disadvantages" with which Cantillon and Adam Smith have made us familiar. But, if we assume that before the bounty was granted there was equilibrium, we must assume that its institution must disturb the equilibrium. The granting of the bounty implies a lowering of the terms on which real income is obtainable in this particular line of enterprise. It is the most elementary implication of the idea of scarcity that if a price is lowered the demand tends to increase.

There is perhaps one refinement of this conclusion which needs to be stated explicitly. It may quite well be that, if the change contemplated is a very small one, no primary movement will take place.[1] Is this in contradiction with our theory? Not at all. The idea of scales of valuation does not assume that every *physical unit* of any of the things which enter into the range of effective valuation must necessarily have a separate significance for action. In the assumption of

[1] By primary movement, I mean movement in the line of production affected; by secondary movement, expansions or contractions of expenditure in other lines. As argued below, some secondary movement is almost inevitable.

the hierarchy of alternatives we do not ignore the fact that, for change to be effective, it must attain the *minimum sensibile*.[1] Changes in price of a penny or twopence may not affect the habits of a given economic subject. But this is not to say that changes of a shilling will not be effective. Nor is it to say that, given limited resources, the necessity of spending more or less on one thing does not *inevitably* affect the distribution of expenditure, even if in the line of expenditure directly affected it leaves the quantity demanded unchanged.[2]

6. Before leaving this part of our subject there is perhaps one further matter which it is desirable to mention explicitly—the relations between the scales of relative valuations and the historical framework of institutions which may be assumed to be existing at any moment. Fortunately, this is not a matter over which it is necessary to linger long, for it has been exhaustively dealt with by Dr. Strigl;[3] and it has never presented great difficulties to those who did not wish to read into Economic Law more than Economic Law actually implies.

The valuation put upon a good by a given economic subject depends essentially upon the qualities of that good and other goods which happen to be in his possession. It follows, therefore, that, in all discussions

---

[1] *Cp.* Wicksteed, *op. cit.*, Part II., chs. i. and ii.

[2] Since we are dealing here with vulgar error, it is perhaps desirable to mention the allegation that the conclusions of economic analysis depend upon the assumption of perfect competition. The answer to this is very short. The allegation is totally wrong. Among the various technical assumptions under which we examine the forms of behaviour imposed by scarcity, free competition is one. But it is only one. Modern economic analysis deals not only with free competition, but with all forms of monopolistic and monopoloid situations. This particular objection, therefore, is a sure indication that the objector does not know what he is talking about.

[3] *Op. cit.*, pp. 85-121.

of tendencies either to equilibrium or to variation, we must start by assuming a given distribution of property. We have seen already how, if distribution changes, relative valuations must be expected to change also.[1] It should be sufficiently clear without further demonstration that all valuations, and hence the whole system of equilibrium analysis, must be understood to start from an initial distribution both of the ultimate commodities and of the command over the factors of production[2] relevant to the situation under discussion.

But this is not all. Given such a distribution of goods and factors, it is clearly necessary to assume a *social order* within which the valuations based upon it may show themselves in tendencies to action. We must assume that there are ways in which this distribution may be altered without external interference, and ways in which it may not. In the theory of simple exchange, for instance, we assume that Primus is free to acquire corn from Secundus by offering him wine. But we do not necessarily assume that he is free to acquire corn by killing him or otherwise doing him violence. We assume a legal framework of economic activity.[3] This framework, as it were, limits by exclusion the area within which the valuations of the economic subjects may influence their action. It prescribes a region in which one is *not* free to adopt all possible expedients; and these prescriptions are assumed in the discussion of what happens in the

[1] See Chapter III., Section 4, above.
[2] This point is made with great clarity by Professor Knight in his review of *Cassel's Theoretische Sozialökonomie* (*Quarterly Journal of Economics*, vol. iii., pp. 279-310); but, of course, it is implicit in the procedure of the whole *corpus* of modern equilibrium analysis.
[3] See J. M. Clark, *The Social Control of Business*, p. 89 *et seq*. In using Professor Clark's phrase, I do not wish to be understood to be endorsing many of the judgments which he passes in this particular connection. See also Cannan, *Wealth*, ch. iv.

residual area of free action. Labour legislation, laws of property and inheritance, tax systems, obstacles to trade and to movement—all these are taken for granted when we assume the scales of relative valuation. We have seen already that these scales assume psychology. It should now be equally clear that they assume institutions.

Thus, from yet another point of view, the relationship between Economic Theory and Economic History, which follows from the main contention of this essay, emerges into prominence. Economic Theory deduces from the assumption of scales of relative valuation their formal implications in different situations. Economic History explains, in terms of all the multitudinous influences at work, the determination of particular economic relationships. If the Economic Theorist, manipulating his shadowy abacus of forms and inevitable relationships, may comfort himself with the reflection that all action must come under its categories, the Economic Historian, too, freed from subservience to other branches of history, may rest assured that there is no segment of the multicoloured weft of events which may not prove relevant to his investigations.

7. It is clear, then, that economic analysis may be conceived to assume the whole structure of "historico-relative" psychology and institutions. It should be equally clear in what respects it can deal with variations in this structure. There are two main ways in which this can be done.

In the first place it can deal with the changes in the distribution of goods which occur as a result of the operation of the equilibrating tendencies. This indeed is the function of the Theory of Equilibrium.

It is to explain movements of this sort that the Theory of Equilibrium is instrumental.

And, secondly, it can *assume* changes in the given structure and describe the difference between the new equilibrium and the old. It can assume the removal of a tax, the imposition of a new obstacle, the effects of a change in certain property relationships. As is well known, this is one of the main functions of the Theory of Variations.

But can it not describe the laws of change in the given data themselves? Can it not tell us how outside these "consequential readjustments"—to use a phrase of Professor Pigou's—the given data themselves change? This raises questions which can be treated more conveniently in another chapter.

CHAPTER V

1. THE scarcity of goods and services, which is the fundamental assumption of the system of deductive generalisations whose nature we have been examining, is a known fact both of introspection and of observation. We know that the means for achieving our own ends are limited; and that, therefore, some ends must be relinquished in favour of the achievement of others. We observe that, faced with a given range of opportunities for the exploitation of which his powers are limited, the creature man prefers some to others; that, at different margins, units of the same class of objects have a different significance for action. And, on the basis of this knowledge, we may assert the applicability of the abstract deductions from the concept

[1] On the main issues discussed in this chapter, the classical works of Senior, Mill, Cairnes, J. N. Keynes, and Menger should be consulted. I have touched very lightly upon the main issues of the old *Methodenstreit*, because I cannot believe that, at this time of day, there is very much to be said about them. So far as I am acquainted with the literature of Institutionalism and "Quantitative Economics" in the spurious sense of this term, nothing has been said by the modern assailants of the traditional methods which was not said in Germany or England fifty or sixty years ago, and no proposition has been advanced which was not finally refuted either by Menger or Max Weber in the thirty years before the War. Hence, in what follows I have addressed myself, not so much to the refutation of error, as to discovering the positive lessons which are to be learnt from the breakdown of the whole movement. The main value of *"Historismus"* and Institutionalism has been to show us more clearly than ever before what claims to avoid.

of scarcity to the actual condition of the world in which we live. Any suggestion that this is not so rests upon the most palpable failure to observe elementary facts. Of course, the existence of scarcity in the sense in which we have defined it is, as it were, an "empirical accident". But, until it can be shown that all the goods, which are the object of human desire, are available in such quantities that no price is obtainable for any one of them and that no human effort, which could have been applied to other desirable ends, is necessary for their reproduction, the persistence of this "empirical accident" may continue to be assumed.

It is sometimes thought that the applicability of economic generalisations has been suspended by the coming of modern machine production. Under primitive conditions, it is urged, the "laws of supply and demand" are no doubt useful and illuminating. But under modern conditions it is different. The coming of the machine changes everything. For the machine-age we need a "new Economics". Such a view involves a complete failure to perceive the nature of the subject-matter of Economics or the scope of its generalisations. It can only be justified in terms of that conception of the economic which we rejected at the outset. It is perfectly true that, with the advance of modern technique, the provision of the most elementary requirements of "material welfare" has come to demand a diminishing proportion of the powers of production at the disposal of the human race. But it is not in the least true that the phenomena of prices and costs, incomes and capitalisation rates, which are the central preoccupation of the Economics of an exchange economy, have

7

shown any tendency to disappear or to lose their practical significance. On the contrary, it is in just these advanced and complicated conditions that the generalisations of Economic Theory are most useful if we are to understand what is happening. Nor has it yet been demonstrated that in any other possible form of society would the general conditions of scarcity cease to have practical relevance.

2. As we have seen already, the generalisations which are deduced from this observation are purely formal in character. If a certain good is scarce, then we know that its disposal must conform to certain laws. If its demand schedule is of a certain order, then we know that with alterations of supply its price must move in a certain way. But, as we have discovered already,[1] there is nothing in this conception of scarcity which warrants us in attaching it to any particular commodity. Our *a priori* deductions do not provide any justification for saying that caviare is an economic good and carrion a disutility. Still less do they inform us concerning the intensity of the demand for caviare or the demand to be rid of carrion. From the point of view of pure Economics these things are conditioned on the one side by individual valuations, and on the other by the technical facts of the given situation. And both individual valuations and technical facts are outside the sphere of economic uniformity. To use Strigl's expressive phrase, from the point of view of economic analysis, these things constitute the *irrational* element in our universe of discourse.[2]

But is it not desirable to transcend such limitations? Ought we not to wish to be in a position to give

---

[1] See above, Chapter II., Sections 1, 2, 3.
[2] Strigl, *op. cit.*, p. 18.

numerical values to the scales of valuation, to establish quantitative laws of demand and supply? This raises, in a slightly different form, the questions we left unanswered at the conclusion of the last chapter.

No doubt such knowledge would be useful. But a moment's reflection should make it plain that we are here entering upon a field of investigation *where there is no reason to suppose that uniformities are to be discovered*. The "causes" which bring it about that the ultimate valuations prevailing at any moment are what they are, are heterogeneous in nature: there is no ground for supposing that the resultant effects should exhibit significant uniformity over time and space. No doubt there is a sense in which it can be argued that every random sample of the universe is the result of determinate causes. But there is no reason to suppose that the study of a random sample of random samples is likely to yield generalisations of any significance. That is not the procedure of the sciences. Yet that, or something very much like it, is the assumption underlying the expectation that the formal categories of economic analysis can be given substantial content of permanent and constant value.[1]

A simple illustration should make this quite clear. Let us take the demand for herrings. Suppose we are confronted with an order fixing the price of herrings at a point below the price hitherto ruling in the market. Suppose we were in a position to say, "According to the researches of Blank (1907-1908) the elasticity of demand for the common herring (*Clupea harengus*) is 1·3; the present price-fixing order therefore may be expected to leave an excess of demand over supply of

---

[1] Note the qualification "permanent and constant value". Before the above conclusion is dismissed as too drastic, the remarks below on the positive value of empirical investigations should be examined.

two million barrels". How pleasant it would be to be able to say things like this! How flattering to our usually somewhat damaged self-esteem *vis-a-vis* the natural scientists! How impressive to big business! How persuasive to the general public!

But can we hope to attain such an enviable position? Let us assume that in 1907-1908 Blank had succeeded in ascertaining that, with a given price change in that year, the elasticity of demand was 1·3. (Rough computations of this sort are not really very difficult.) What reason is there to suppose that he was unearthing a constant law? No doubt the herring meets certain physiological needs which are capable of fairly accurate description, although it is by no means the only food capable of meeting these needs. The demand for herrings, however, is not a simple derivative of needs. It is, as it were, a function of a great many apparently independent variables. It is a function of fashion; and by fashion is meant something more than the ephemeral results of an Eat British Herrings campaign; the demand for herrings might be substantially changed by a change in the theological views of the economic subjects entering the market. It is a function of the availability of other foods. It is a function of the quantity and quality of the population. It is a function of the distribution of income within the community and of changes in the volume of money. Transport changes will alter the area of demand for herrings. Discoveries in the art of cooking may change their relative desirability. Is it possible reasonably to suppose that coefficients derived from the observation of a particular herring market at a particular time and place have any *permanent* significance—save as Economic History?

Now, of course, by the aid of various devices it is possible to extend the area of observation over periods of time. Instead of observing the market for herrings for a few days, statistics of price changes and changes in supply and demand may be collected over a period of years and by judicious "doctoring" for seasonal movements, population change, and so on, be used to deduce a figure representing average elasticity over the period.[1] And within limits such computations have their uses. They are a convenient way of describing certain forces operative during that period of history. As we shall see later on, they may provide some guidance concerning what may happen in the immediate future. But they have no claim to be regarded as "laws". However accurately they describe the past, there is no presumption that they will describe the future. Things have just happened to be so in the past. They may continue to be so for a short time in the future. But there is no reason to suppose that their having been so in the past is the result of the operation of homogeneous causes, nor that their changes in the future will be due to the causes which have operated in the past. Important as such investigations may be, at the moment at which they are made and perhaps for a short time after, there is no justification for claiming for their results the status of the so-called "statistical" laws of the natural sciences.[2]

3. If this is true of attempts to provide definite quantitative values for such elementary concepts as demand and supply functions, how much more does

[1] See, e.g., Schultz, *The Statistical Laws of Demand and Supply*; Leontieff, *Ein Versuch zur Statistischen Analyse von Angebot und Nachfrage (Weltwirtschaftliches Archiv)*, vol. xxx., p. ix *seq.*; Staehle, *Die Analyse von Nachfragekurven in ihrer Bedeutung für die Konjunkturforschung.*

[2] On the problems discussed above very interesting remarks are to be found in Halberstaédter, *Die Problematik des Wirtschaftlichen Prinzips.*

it apply to attempts to provide "concrete" laws of the movement of more complex phenomena, price fluctuations, cost dispersions, business cycles, and the like. In the last ten years there has been a great multiplication of this sort of thing under the name of Institutionalism, "Quantitative Economics", "Dynamic Economics", and what not;[1] yet most of the investigations involved have been doomed to futility from the outset and might just as well never have been undertaken. The theory of probability on which modern mathematical statistics is based affords no justification for averaging where conditions are obviously not such as to warrant the belief that homogeneous causes of different kinds are operating. Yet this is the normal procedure of much of the work of this kind. The correlation of trends subject to influences of the most diverse character is scrutinised for "quantitative laws". Averages are taken of phenomena occurring under the most heterogeneous circumstances of time and space, and the result is expected to have significance. In Professor Wesley Mitchell's *Business Cycles*,[2] for instance, a work for whose collection of data economists are rightly grateful, after a prolonged and valuable account of the course of business fluctuations in different countries since the end of the eighteenth century, an average is struck of the duration of all cycles and a Logarithmic Normal Curve is fitted by

[1] On the aspect of Institutionalism discussed below, Professor Wesley Mitchell's essay on *The Prospects of Economics* in the *Trend of Economics* (edited Tugwell) should be consulted. On the general position of the school, see Morgenstern, *Bemerkungen über die Problematik der Amerikanischen Institutionalisten* in the *Suggi di Storia e Teori Economica in onore e recordo di Giuseppe Prato*, Turin, 1931; Fetter, art. America, *Wirtschaftstheorie der Gegenwart*, Bd. 1, pp. 31-60. See also the review of the *Trend of Economics* by the late Professor Allyn Young, reprinted in his *Economic Problems New and Old*, pp. 232-260.

[2] *Business Cycles*, 2nd edition, p. 419.

Davies' Method to the frequency distribution of the 166 observations involved. What possible meaning can inhere in such an operation? Here are observations of conditions widely differing in time, space, and the institutional framework of business activity. If there is any significance at all in bringing them together, it must be by way of *contrast*. Yet Professor Mitchell, who never tires of belittling the methods and results of orthodox analysis, apparently thinks that, by taking them all together and fitting a highly complicated curve to their frequency distribution, he is constructing something significant—something which is more than a series of straight lines and curves on half a page of his celebrated treatise.[1] Certainly he has provided the most mordant comment on the methodology of "Quantitative Economics" that any of its critics could possibly wish.

There is no need to linger on the futility of these grandiose projects. After all, in spite of their recent popularity, they are not new, and a movement which has continually invoked a pragmatic logic may well be judged by a pragmatic test. It is just about a hundred years ago since Richard Jones, in his Inaugural Lecture at King's College, London,[2] sounded

[1] On this see Morgenstern, *International Vergleichende Konjunkturforschung* (*Zeitschrift für die Gesammte Staatswissenschaft*, vol.lxxxiii,. p.261). In the second edition of his book, Professor Mitchell attempts to meet Dr. Morgenstern's strictures in an extensive footnote, but so far as I can see, beyond urging that his observations for China relate to coast towns (!), he does not go beyond a dogmatic reiteration that "the distribution of the observations around their central tendency is a matter of much theoretical interest" (*Business Cycles*, 2nd edition, p. 420).

[2] Richard Jones, *Collected Works*, pp. 21 and 22. The comparison is not altogether fair to Jones, who in some ways had a real contribution to make to Economics. The true precursor of modern "Quantitative Economics" was Sir Josiah Child, who attempted to prove that the concomitance of low interest rates and great riches was an indication that the latter was the result of the former.

the note of revolt against the "formal abstraction" of Ricardian Economics, with arguments which, if more vividly expressed, are more or less exactly similar to those which have been expressed by the advocates of "inductive methods" ever since that day. And time has gone on, and the "rebels" have become a highly respectable band of expert authorities, the pontifical occupants of chairs, the honoured recipients of letters from the Kaiser, the directing functionaries of expensive research institutes. . . . We have had the Historical School. And now we have the Institutionalists. Save in one or two privileged places, it is safe to say that, until the close of the War, views of this sort were dominant in German University circles; and in recent years, if they have not secured the upper hand altogether, they have certainly had a wide area of power in America. Yet not one single "law" deserving of the name, not one quantitative generalisation of permanent validity has emerged from their efforts. A certain amount of interesting statistical material. Many useful monographs on particular historical situations. But of "concrete laws", substantial uniformities of "economic behaviour", not one. And, at the end of the hundred years, the greatest slump in history finds them sterile and incapable of helpful comment—their trends gone awry and their dispersions distorted.[1] Meanwhile, a few isolated thinkers, using the despised apparatus of deductive theory, have brought our knowledge of the theory of

---

[1] The discredit of the Historical School in Germany is very largely due to the failure of its members to understand the currency disturbances of the War and the post-War period. It is not improbable that the utter failure of "Quantitative Economics" to understand or predict the great slump may be followed by a similar revulsion. It would certainly be difficult to imagine a more complete or more conspicuous exposure.

fluctuations to a point from which the fateful events
of the last few years can be explained in general terms,
and a complete solution of the riddle of depressions
within the next few years does not seem outside the
bounds of probability.

4. But what, then, are we to say of empirical
studies? Having ascertained the persistence of the
fact of scarcity, is the economist then excused from
the obligation of maintaining further contact with
reality?

The answer is most decidedly in the negative.
And the negative answer is implicit in the practice of
all those economists who, since Adam Smith and
Cantillon, have contributed most to the development
of Economic Science. It has never been the case that
the exponents of the so-called orthodox tradition have
frowned upon empirical studies. As Menger pointed
out years ago, at the height of the *Methodenstreit*,[1]
the analytical school have never been the assailants
in these controversies. The attacks, the attempts to
exclude, have always come from the other side. The
analytics have always acknowledged the importance
of realistic studies, and have themselves contributed
much to the development of the technique of such
investigations. Indeed, it may be argued that the
most important work of this kind has come, not from
this or that "rebel" group who were calling in question
the application in Economics of the elementary laws
of thought, but rather from just those men who were
the object of their onslaught. In the history of Applied
Economics, the work of a Jevons, a Taussig, a Bowley,
has more claim on our attention than the work of,
say, a Schmoller, a Veblen, or a Hamilton. And this

[1] *Die Inthümer des Historismus,* Preface, pp. iii. and iv.

is no accident. The fruitful conduct of realistic studies can only be undertaken by those who have a firm grasp of analytical principle and some notion of what can and what cannot legitimately be expected from activities of this sort.

But what, then, are legitimate expectations in this respect?

The first and the most obvious is the provision of a check on the applicability to given situations of different types of theoretical constructions. As we have seen already, the *truth* of a particular theory is a matter of its logical derivation from the general assumptions of the science. But its *applicability* to a given situation depends upon the extent to which its concepts actually reflect the forces operating in that situation. Now the concrete manifestations of scarcity are various and changing; and, unless there is continuous check on the words which are used to describe them, there is always a danger that the area of application of a particular principle may be misconceived. The terminology of theory and the terminology of practice, although apparently identical, may, in fact, cover different areas.

A simple illustration will make this clear. According to pure monetary theory, if the quantity of money in circulation is increased and other things remain the same, the value of money must fall. As we have seen, this is deducible from the elementary categories of the science, and its truth is independent of further inductive test. But its applicability to a given situation depends upon a correct understanding of what things are to be regarded as money, and this is a matter which can only be discovered by reference back to the facts. It may well be that over a period of time the concrete significance of the term "money" has altered. If then, while retaining the original term, we proceed to interpret a new situation in terms of the original content, we may be led into serious misapprehension. We may even conclude that the *theory* is fallacious. It is indeed well known that this has happened again and again in the course of the history of theory. The failure of the Currency School to secure permanent acceptance for their theory of Banking and the Exchanges, in other respects so greatly superior to that of their opponents, was notoriously due to their failure to perceive the importance of including Bank Credit in their conception of money. Only by continuous sifting and scrutiny of the changing body of facts[1] can such misapprehensions be avoided.

But, secondly, we may expect of realistic studies, not merely a knowledge of the appropriate application of particular theories, but also the exposure of areas where pure theory needs to be reformulated and extended. Empirical studies bring to light new problems.

The best example of the unexplained residue is provided by those fluctuations of trade which have come to be known as the trade cycle. Pure equilibrium theory, as is well known, does not provide any explanation of the phenomena of booms and slumps. It explains the adjustment of the economic system to external change either on the demand side or on the supply side. It explains fluctuations which are in the nature of orderly adaptations. But it does not explain the existence within the economic system of tendencies conducive to disproportionate development. It does not explain discrepancies between total supply

[1] Professor Jacob Viner's *Canadian Balance of International Indebtedness* and Professor Taussig's *International Trade* provide classic examples of this kind of investigation.

and total demand in the sense in which these terms are used in the celebrated Law of Markets.[1] Yet unquestionably such discrepancies exist, and any attempt to interpret reality solely in terms of such a theory must necessarily leave a residue of phenomena not capable of being subsumed under its generalisations.

Here is a clear case where empirical studies bring us face to face with the insufficiencies of certain generalisations. And it is in the revelation of deficiencies of this kind that the main function of realistic studies in relation to theory consists.[2] The theoretical economist who wishes to safeguard the implications of his theory must be continually "trying out", in the explanation of particular situations, the generalisations he has already achieved. It is in the examination of particular instances that lacunæ in the structure of existing theory tend to be revealed.

But this is not in the least to say that the *solution* of the problems thus presented are themselves to be discovered by the mere multiplication of observations of divergences of this sort. That is not the function of observation, and the whole history of the various "inductive revolts" shows that all studies based on this expectation have proved utterly fruitless. This is particularly true of trade cycle theory. So long as the investigators of this problem were content with the multiplication of time series and the accumulation of coefficients of correlation, no significant advance was discernible. It was not until there arose men who were prepared to undertake the entirely different task of starting where equilibrium analysis leaves off and

---

[1] On all this see Hayek, *Geldtheorie und Konjunkturtheorie*, Kap. i. and ii., *passim*.

[2] Another important function, this time in relation to practice, will be discussed in the next section.

deriving from the pure categories of pure theory an explanation of fluctuation which is compatible with the assumptions of that analysis, that progress began to be made. There can be no better example of the correct relationship between the two branches of study. Realistic studies may suggest the problem to be solved. They may test the range of applicability of the answer when it is forthcoming. But it is theory and theory alone which is capable of supplying the solution. Any attempt to reverse the relationship must lead inevitably to the nirvana of purposeless observation and record.

Moreover—and this brings us back to the point from which we started—there is no reason to believe that the generalisations which may be elaborated to explain the residues thus discovered will be anything but formal in character. For reasons which we have already examined, the hope of giving permanent and substantial content to the categories of pure analysis is vain. By "trying out" pure theory on concrete situations and referring back to pure theory residual difficulties, we may hope continually to improve and extend our analytical apparatus. But that such studies should enable us to say what goods must be economic goods and what precise values will be attached to them in different situations, is not to be expected. To say this is not to abandon the hope of solving any genuine problem of Economics. It is merely to recognise what does and what does not lie within the necessary boundaries of our subject-matter. To pretend that this is not so is just pseudo-scientific bravado.

5. But to recognise that Economic laws are formal in nature is not to deny the reality of the necessi-

ties they describe or to derogate from their value as a means of interpretation and prediction. On the contrary, having carefully delimited the nature and the scope of such generalisations, we may proceed with all the greater confidence to claim for them a complete necessity within this field.

Economic laws describe inevitable implications. If the data they postulate are given, then the consequences they predict necessarily follow. In this sense, as Professor Knight emphasises, they are as universal as the laws of mathematics or mechanics,[1] and as little capable of "suspension". If, in a given situation, the facts are of a certain order, Economic law warrants us in deducing with complete certainty that other facts which it enables us to describe are also present. To those who have grasped the implications of the proposition set forth in the last chapter the reason is not far to seek. If the "given situation" conforms to a certain pattern, certain other features must also be present, for their presence is "deducible" from the pattern originally postulated. The analytic method is simply a way of discovering the necessary consequences of complex collocations of facts—consequences whose counterpart in reality is not so immediately discernible as the counterpart of the original postulates. It is an instrument for "shaking out" all the implications of given suppositions. It is a form of applied logic, and, granted the correspondence of its original assumptions and the facts, its conclusions are inevitable and inescapable.

All this becomes particularly clear if we consider the procedure of diagrammatic analysis. Suppose, for

[1] *Scientific Method in Economics* (essay in *The Trend of Economics*, edited Tugwell, p. 256).

example, we wish to exhibit the effects on price of the imposition of a small tax. We make certain suppositions as regards the elasticity of demand, certain suppositions as regards the cost functions, embody these in the usual diagram, and we can at once *read off*, as it were, the effects on the price.[1] They are implied in the original suppositions. The diagram has simply made explicit the concealed implications.

It is this inevitability of economic analysis which gives it its very considerable prognostic value. It has been emphasised sufficiently already that Economic Science knows no way of predicting what will be the given data at any particular point of time. It cannot predict changes of valuations. But, given the data in a particular situation, it can draw inevitable conclusions as to their implications. And if the data remain unchanged, these implications will certainly be realised. They must be, for they are implied in the presence of the original data.

It is just here that we can perceive yet a further function for empirical investigation. It can bring to light the changing facts which make prediction in any given situation possible. As we have seen, it is most improbable that it can ever discover the law of their change, for the data are not subject to homogeneous causal influences. But it can put us in possession of information which is relevant at the particular moment concerned. It can give us some idea of the relative magnitude of the different forces operative. It can afford a basis for enlightened conjectures with regard to potential directions of change. And this unquestionably is one of the main uses of applied studies—not to unearth empirical laws in an area

---

[1] See, *e.g.*, Dalton, *Public Finance*, 2nd edition, p. 73.

where the rule of law is not to be expected, but to
provide from moment to moment some knowledge of
the varying data on which, in the given situation,
prediction can be based. It cannot supersede formal
analysis. But it can suggest in different situations
what formal analysis is appropriate, and it can provide
at that moment some content for the formal categories.

Of course, if other things do not remain unchanged,
the consequences predicted do not necessarily follow.
This elementary platitude, necessarily implicit in *any*
scientific prediction, needs especially to be kept in
the foreground of attention when discussing this kind
of prognosis. The statesman who said *"Ceteris paribus
be damned !"*, has a large and enthusiastic following
among the critics of Economics! Nobody in his senses
would hold that the laws of mechanics were invalidated if an experiment designed to illustrate them
were interrupted by an earthquake. Yet a substantial
majority of the lay public, and a good many *soi-disant*
economists as well, are continually criticising well-
established economic laws on grounds hardly less
slender.[1] A protective tariff is imposed on the im-

---

[1] See, *e.g.*, the various statistical "refutations" of the quantity theory
of money which have appeared in recent years. On all these the classic
comment of Torrens on Tooke is the last word that need ever be uttered.
"The History of Prices may be regarded as a psychological study. Mr. Tooke
commenced his labours as a follower of Horner and Ricardo, and derived
reflected lustre from an alliance with those celebrated names; but his
capacity for collecting contemporaneous facts preponderating over his
perceptive and logical faculties, his accumulation of facts involved him in a
labyrinth of error. Failing to perceive that a theoretical principle, although
it may irresistibly command assent under all circumstances coinciding
with the premises from which it is deduced, must be applied with due
limitation and correction in all cases not coinciding with the premises, he
fell into a total misconception of the proposition advanced by Adam Smith,
and imputed to that high authority the absurdity of maintaining that
variations in the quantity of money cause the money values of all commodities to vary in equal proportions, while the values of commodities,
in relation to each other, are varying in unequal proportions. Reasonings
derived from this extraordinary misconception necessarily led to extra-

portation of commodities, the conditions of whose
domestic production makes it certain that, if other
things remain unchanged, the effect of such protection
will be a rise in price. For quite adventitious reasons,
the progress of technique, the lowering of the price of
raw materials, wage reductions, or what not, costs are
reduced and the price does not rise. In the eyes of
the lay public and "Institutionalist" economists the
generalisations of Economics are invalidated. The
laws of supply and demand are suspended. The
bogus claims of a science which does not regard the
facts are laid bare. And so on and so forth. Yet,
whoever asked of the practitioners of any other
science that they should predict the complete course
of an uncontrolled history?

Now, no doubt, the very fact that events in the
large are uncontrolled,[1] that the fringe of given data

---

ordinary conclusions. Having satisfied himself that Adam Smith had
correctly established as a principle universally true that variations in the
purchasing power of money cause the prices of all commodities to vary in
equal proportions, and finding, as he pursued his investigations into the
phenomena of the market at different periods, no instances in which an
expansion or contraction of the circulation caused the prices of commodities
to rise or fall in an equal ratio, he arrived by a strictly logical inference from
the premises thus illogically assumed, at his grand discovery—that no
increase of the circulating medium can have the effect of increasing prices"
(*The Principles and Operation of Sir Robert Peel's Act of* 1844 *Explained
and Defended*, 1st edition, p. 75).

[1] The alleged advantage of economic "planning"—namely, that it
enables greater certainty with regard to the future—depends upon the
assumption that under "planning" the present controlling forces, the
choices of individual spenders and savers, are themselves brought under the
control of the planners. The paradox therefore arises that either the planner
is destitute of the instrument of calculating the ends of the community he
intends to serve, or, if he restores the instrument, he removes the *raison
d'être* of the "plan". Of course, the dilemma does not arise if he thinks
himself capable of interpreting these ends or—what is much more probable—
if he has no intention of serving any other ends but those *he* thinks appropriate. Strange to say this not infrequently happens. Scratch a would-be
planner and you usually find a would-be dictator.

is so extensive and so exposed to influence from
unexpected quarters, must make the task of prediction, however carefully safeguarded, extremely hazard-
ous. In many situations, small changes in particular
groups of data are so liable to be counterbalanced by
other changes which may be occurring independently
and simultaneously, that the prognostic value of the
knowledge of operative tendencies is small. But there
are certain broad changes, usually involving many
lines of expenditure or production at once, where a
knowledge of implications is a very firm basis for conjectures of strong probability. This is particularly the
case in the sphere of monetary phenomena. There
can be no question that a quite elementary knowledge
of the Quantity Theory was immense prognostic
value during the War and the disturbances which
followed. If the speculators who bought German
marks, after the War, in the confident expectation
that the mark would automatically resume its old
value, had been aware of as much of the theory of
money as was known, say, to Sir William Petty, they
would have known that what they were doing was
ridiculous. Similarly, it becomes more and more
clear, for purely analytical reasons, that, once the
signs of a major boom in trade have made their
appearance, the coming of slump and depression is
almost certain; though when it will come and how long
it will last are not matters which are predictable,
since they depend upon human volitions occurring
after the indications in question have appeared. So,
too, in the sphere of the labour market, it is quite
certain that some types of wage policy must result
in unemployment if other things remain equal: and
knowledge of how the "other things" must change

in order that this consequence may be avoided makes it very often possible to predict with considerable confidence the actual results of given policies. These things have been verified again and again in practice. Today it is only he who is blind because he does not want to see who is prepared to deny their validity. If certain conditions are present, then certain consequences are inevitable.

6. None the less, economic laws have their limits, and, if we are to use them wisely, it is important that we should realise exactly wherein these limitations consist. In the light of what has been said already, this should not be difficult.

The irrational element in the economist's universe of discourse lies behind the individual valuation. As we have seen already, there is no means available for determining the probable movement of the relative scales of valuation. Hence in all our analysis we take the scales of valuation as given. It is only what follows from these given assumptions that has the character of inevitability. It is only in this area that we find the régime of law.

It follows, therefore, that economic laws cannot be held to relate to movements of the relative scales, and that economic causation only extends through the range of their original implication. This is not to say that changes in values may not be contemplated. Of course, changes in values are the main preoccupation of theoretical Economics. It is only to say that, as economists, we cannot go behind changes in individual valuations. To put the matter in less abstract terms, we may explain, in terms of economic law, price-relationships which follow from given technical conditions and relative valuations. We may explain changes due to changes in these data. But we cannot explain changes in the data themselves. To demarcate these types of change the Austrians[1] distinguish between endogenous and exogenous changes. The ones occur within a given structure of assumptions. The others come from outside.

We can see the relevance of these distinctions to the problem of prognosis if we consider once more the implications of the theory of money. Given certain assumptions with regard to the demand for money, we are justified in asserting that an increase in the volume of any currency will be followed by a fall in its external value. This is an endogenous change. It follows from the original assumptions, and, so long as they hold, it is clearly inevitable. We are not justified in asserting, however, as has been so often asserted in recent years, that if the exchanges fall, inflation *must* necessarily follow. We know that very often this happens. We know that governments are often foolish and craven and that false views of the functions of money are widely prevalent. But there is no *inevitable* connection between a fall in the exchanges and a decision to set the printing presses working. A new human volition interrupts the chain of "causation". But between the issue of paper money and the fall in its external value, no change in the assumed disposition to action on the part of the various economic subjects concerned is contemplated. All that happens is, as it were, that the exchange index moves to a lower level.

A more complicated example of the same distinction is provided by the Reparations controversy.

---

[1] See especially Strigl, *Aenderungen in den Daten der Wirtschaft* (*Jahrbücher für Nationalökonomie und Statistik*, vol. cxxviii., pp. 641-662).

Suppose that it could be shown that the external demand for German products was very inelastic, so that in the short period, at any rate, the degree of necessary transfer burden over and above the burden of paying the domestic taxes was very great. In such circumstances it might be argued that the present crisis was directly due to purely economic factors. That is to say that, up to the point at which panic supervened, the various complications were entirely due to obstacles implicit in the given conditions of world supply and demand.[1] But suppose it can be shown that the prime cause of the present difficulty was financial panic, induced by the fear of political revolt at the magnitude of the original tax burden, then it cannot be argued that the train of causation was wholly economic. The political reaction to the tax burden intervenes. The "transfer crisis" arises from exogenous causes.

Now there can be no doubt that in the discussion of practical problems, certain kinds of exogenous changes, apparently closely connected with changes within the chain of economic causation, are not infrequently involved. In the sphere of monetary problems the danger that falling exchanges may induce the monetary authorities of the area involved to embark on inflation, will certainly be considered germane to the discussion. In the sphere of tariff policy, the tendency of the granting of a protective tariff to create monopolistic communities of interest among domestic producers is certainly a probability which should not be overlooked by the practical administrator. Here and in many other connections there

---

[1] This is the limiting case discussed in Dr. Machlup's *Transfer und Preisbewegung* (*Zeitschrift für Nationalökonomie*, vol. i., pp. 555-561).

is a penumbra of psychological probabilities which, for purely practical reasons, it is often very convenient to take into account.[1] No doubt the kind of insight required into these problems is often of a very elementary order—although it is surprising how many people lack it. No doubt most of the probabilities involved are virtual certainties. The proposition, for instance, that if it is made possible for democratic politicians to offer political bribes, some of them will sometimes do it, does not seem much more disputable than the proposition that the sun will rise tomorrow. Men in possession of their senses are not likely to question it as a working maxim of political practice. Still, not all participants in discussions of this sort are in possession of their senses, and it is highly desirable that every effort should be made to keep separate, at any rate in mode of statement,[2] those generalisations which have the character of certainty, which are Economic Generalisations proper, from those generalisations of the "sociological penumbra", which only

[1] Into the same category fall the much more difficult questions relating to the influence of changing incomes on birth-rates, etc. The population problem as a whole is one of the most conspicuous residents of this borderland of applied Economics.

[2] The qualification is important. It is more accuracy in mode of statement, not over-austerity in speculative range for which I am pleading. I am very far from suggesting that, when discussing practical problems, economists should refrain from contemplating the probability of those changes in the data whose causation falls outside the strict limits of Economic Science. Indeed, I am inclined to believe that there is here a field of sociological speculation in which economists may have a definite advantage over others. Certainly it is a field in which hitherto they have done very much more than others—one has only to think of the various discussions of the possible forms of a Tariff Commission in a democratic community (e.g., Plant, *Tariffs in Practice; Tariffs, the Case Restated*, edited by Sir William Beveridge) or the necessary conditions of bureaucratic administration of productive enterprise (e.g., Mises, *Die Gemeinwirtschaft*, pp. 199-210) to see the sort of thing I have in mind. All that I am contending is the desirability of separating out the kind of generalisation which belongs to this field from the kind which belongs to Economics proper.

have a high degree of probability. Economists have nothing to lose by underlining the limitations of Economic Law. Indeed, it is only when this is done that the overwhelming power to convince of what remains can be expected to have free play.

CHAPTER VI

1. WE now approach the last stage of our investigations. We have surveyed the subject-matter of Economics. We have examined the nature of its generalisations and their bearing on the interpretation of Reality. We have finally to ask: What is the significance of it all for social life and conduct ? What is the bearing of Economic Science on practice?

2. It is sometimes thought that certain developments in modern Economic Theory furnish *by themselves* a set of norms capable of providing a basis for political practice. The Law of Diminishing Marginal Utility is held to provide a criterion of all forms of political and social activity affecting distribution. Anything conducive to greater equality, which does not adversely affect production, is said to be justified by this law; anything conducive to inequality, condemned. These propositions have received the support of very high authority. They are the basis of much that is written on the Theory of Public Finance.[1] No less an authority than Professor Cannan has invoked them, to justify the ways of economists to Fabian Socialists.[2] They have received the widest countenance in number-

[1] See, *e.g.*, Edgeworth, *The Pure Theory of Taxation (Papers Relating to Political Economy*, vol. ii., p. 63 *seq.*).

[2] See *Economics and Socialism (The Economic Outlook*, pp. 59-62).

less works on Applied Economics. It is safe to say that the great majority of English economists accept them as axiomatic. Yet with great diffidence I venture to suggest that they are in fact entirely unwarranted by any doctrine of scientific economics, and that outside this country they have very largely ceased to hold sway.

The argument by which these propositions are supported is familiar: but it is worth while repeating it explicitly in order to show the exact points at which it is defective. The Law of Diminishing Marginal Utility implies that the more one has of anything the less one values additional units thereof. Therefore, it is said, the more real income one has, the less one values additional units of income. Therefore the marginal utility of a rich man's income is less than the marginal utility of a poor man's income. Therefore, if transfers are made, and these transfers do not appreciably affect production, total utility will be increased. Therefore, such transfers are "economically justified". *Quod erat demonstrandum.*

At first sight the plausibility of the argument is overwhelming. But on closer inspection it is seen to be merely specious. It rests upon an extension of the Law of Diminishing Marginal Utility into a field in which it is entirely illegitimate. The "Law of Diminishing Marginal Utility" here invoked does not follow in the least from the fundamental conception of economic goods; and it makes assumptions which, whether they are true or false, can never be verified by observation or introspection. The proposition we are examining begs the great metaphysical question of the scientific comparability of different individual experiences. This deserves further examination.

The Law of Diminishing Marginal Utility, as we have seen, is derived from the conception of a scarcity of means in relation to the ends which they serve. It assumes that, for each individual, goods can be ranged in order of their significance for conduct; and that, in the sense that it will be preferred, we can say that one use of a good is more important than another. Proceeding on this basis, we can compare the order in which one individual may be supposed to prefer certain alternatives with the order in which they are preferred by another individual. In this way it is possible to build up a complete theory of exchange.

But it is one thing to assume that scales can be drawn up showing the *order* in which an individual will prefer a series of alternatives, and to compare the arrangement of one such individual scale with another. It is quite a different thing to assume that behind such arrangements lie magnitudes which themselves can be compared as between individual scales. This is not an assumption which need anywhere be made in modern economic analysis, and it is an assumption which is of an entirely different kind from the assumption of individual scales of relative valuation. The theory of exchange assumes that I can compare the importance *to me* of Bread at 6d. per loaf and 6d. spent on other alternatives presented by the opportunities of the market, or—to empty out even the explanatory assumption of introspection—it assumes that confronted with such opportunities in certain circumstances my response will be of a determinate nature. And it assumes that the order of my preferences thus exhibited can be compared with the order of preferences of the Baker. But it does *not* assume that, at any point, it is necessary to compare the satisfaction which I get from the spending of 6d. on bread with the satisfaction which *the Baker* gets by receiving it. That comparison is a comparison of an entirely different nature. It is a comparison which is never needed in the theory of equilibrium and which is never implied by the assumptions of that theory. It is a comparison which necessarily falls outside the scope of any positive science. To state that A's preference stands above B's in order of importance is entirely different from stating that A prefers *n* to *m* and B prefers *n* and *m* in a different order. It involves an element of conventional valuation. Hence it is essentially normative. It has no place in pure science.

If this is still obscure, the following considerations should be decisive. Suppose that a difference of opinion were to arise about A's preferences. Suppose that I thought that, at certain prices, he preferred *n* to *m*, and you thought that, at the same prices, he preferred *m* to *n*. It would be easy to settle our differences in a purely scientific manner. Either we could ask A to tell us. Or, if we refused to believe that introspection on A's part was possible, we could expose him to the stimuli in question and observe his behaviour. Either test would be such as to provide the basis for a settlement of the difference of opinion.

But suppose that we differed about the satisfaction derived by A from an income of £1,000, and the satisfaction derived by B from an income of twice that magnitude. Asking them would provide no solution. Supposing they differed. A might urge that he had more satisfaction than B at the margin. While B might urge that, on the contrary, he had more satisfaction than A. We do not need to be slavish behaviourists to realise that here is no scientific evidence. *There is no means of testing the magnitude of A's satisfaction as compared with B's.* If we tested the state of their blood-streams, that would be a test of blood, not satisfaction. Introspection does not enable A to discover what is going on in B's mind, nor B to discover what is going on in A's. There is no way of comparing the satisfactions of different people.

Now, of course, in daily life we do continually assume that the comparison can be made. But the very diversity of the assumptions actually made at different times and in different places is evidence of their conventional nature. In Western democracies we assume for certain purposes that men in similar circumstances are capable of equal satisfactions. Just as for purposes of justice we assume equality of responsibility in similar situations as between legal subjects, so for purposes of public finance we agree to assume equality of capacity for experiencing satisfaction from equal incomes in similar circumstances as between economic subjects. But, although it may be convenient to assume this, there is no way of proving that the assumption rests on ascertainable fact. And, indeed, if the representative of some other civilisation were to assure us that we were wrong, that members of his caste were capable of experiencing ten times as much satisfaction from given incomes as members of an inferior caste, we could not refute him. We might poke fun at him. We might flare up with indignation, and say that his valuation was hateful, that it led to civil strife, unhappiness, unjust privilege, and so on and so forth. But we could not show that he was wrong in any objective sense, any more than we could show that we were right. And since in our hearts we do not believe that men are equally capable of satisfaction, it would really be rather silly if we continued to pretend that the justification for our scheme of things was in any way *scientific*. It can be justified on grounds of general convenience. Or it can be justified by appeal to ultimate standards of value. But it cannot be justified by appeal to any kind of positive science.

Hence the extension of the Law of Diminishing Marginal Utility, postulated in the propositions we are examining, is entirely illegitimate. And the arguments based upon it therefore are all lacking in scientific foundation. Recognition of this no doubt involves a substantial curtailment of the claims of much of what now assumes the status of scientific generalisation in current discussions of applied Economics. The Law of Diminishing Marginal Utility does not justify the inference that transferences from the rich to the poor will increase total satisfaction. It does not tell us that a graduated income tax is less injurious to the social dividend than a non-graduated poll tax. Indeed, all that part of the theory of Public Finance which deals with "Social Utility" goes by the board. Interesting as a development of an ethical postulate, it is entirely foreign to the assumptions of scientific Economics. It is simply the accidental deposit of the historical association of English Economics with Utilitarianism: and both the utilitarian postulates from which it derives and the analytical Economics with which it has been associated will be the better and the more convincing for the separation.[1]

[1] Cp. Davenport, *Value and Distribution*, pp. 301 and 571; Benham, *Economic Welfare (Economica*, June, 1930, pp. 173-187); M. Ste. Braun, *Theorie der Staatlichen Wirtschaftspolitik*, pp. 41-44. Even Professor Irving Fisher, anxious to provide a justification for his highly ingenious but entirely question-begging statistical method for measuring "marginal utility", can find no better apology for his procedure than that "Philosophic doubt is

But supposing this were not so. Suppose that we could bring ourselves to tolerate the intrusion of these conventional assumptions that individual experiences can be compared, and that one man is as capable of experiencing satisfaction as another. And suppose that, proceeding on this basis, we had succeeded in showing that certain policies *had the effect* of increasing "social utility", even so it would be totally illegitimate to argue that such a conclusion by itself warranted the inference that these policies *ought* to be carried out. For such an inference would beg the whole question whether the increase of satisfaction in this sense was socially obligatory.[1] And there is nothing within the body of economic generalisations, even thus enlarged by the inclusion of elements of conventional valuation, which affords any means of deciding this question. Propositions involving "ought" are on an entirely different plane from propositions involving "is". But more of this later.[2]

---

right and proper, but the problems of life cannot and do not wait" (*Economic Essays in Honour of John Bates Clark*, p. 180). It does not seem to me that the problem of measuring marginal utility as between individuals is a particularly pressing problem. But whether this is so or not, the fact remains that Professor Fisher solves his problem only by making a conventional assumption. And it does not seem that it anywhere aids the solution of practical problems to pretend that conventional assumptions have scientific justification. It does not make me a more docile democrat to be told that *I* am equally capable of experiencing satisfaction as my neighbour; it fills me with unutterable fury. But I am perfectly willing to accept the statement that it is *convenient* to assume that this is the case. I am quite willing to accept the argument that in modern conditions societies which proceed on any other assumption have an inherent instability. But we are past the days when democracy could be made acceptable by the pretence that judgments of value are judgments of scientific `fact. (For a detailed discussion of the Fisher proposals, see A. Bilimovic, *Irving Fisher's statistische Methode für die Bemessung des Grenznutzens* [*Zeitschrift für Nationalökonomie*, Bd. 1, pp. 114-129].)

[1] Psychological hedonism in so far as it went beyond the individual may have involved a non-scientific assumption, but it was not by itself a necessary justification for ethical hedonism.

[2] See below, Section 4.

3. Exactly the same type of stricture may be applied to any attempt to make the criteria of free equilibrium in the price system at the same time the criteria of "economic justification". The pure theory of equilibrium enables us to understand how, given the valuations of the various economic subjects and the facts of the legal and technical environment, a system of relationships can be conceived towards which existing relationships may be regarded as tending. It enables us to describe that distribution of resources which, given the valuations of the individual concerned, satisfies demand most fully. But it does not by itself provide any ethical sanctions. To show that, under certain conditions, demand is satisfied more adequately than under any alternative set of conditions, does not prove that that set of conditions is desirable. There is no penumbra of approbation round the Theory of Equilibrium. Equilibrium is just equilibrium.

Now, of course, given the desirability of individual liberty, absence of regimentation, power of continuous initiative, there is strong reason for supposing that conformity to the criteria of free economic equilibrium constitutes a fulfilment of these norms.[1] It is of the essence of the conception of equilibrium that, given his initial resources, each individual secures a range of free choice, bounded only by the limitations of the material environment and the exercise of a similar freedom on the part of the other economic subjects. In equilibrium each individual is free to move to a different point on his lines of preference, but he does

[1] See two very important papers by Professor Plant, *Co-ordination and Competition in Transport* (*Journal of the Institute of Transport*, vol. xiii., pp. 127-136); *Trends in Business Administration* (*Economica*, No. 35, pp. 45-62).

not move, for, in the circumstances postulated, any other point would be less preferred. But freedom to choose may not be regarded as an ultimate good. The creation of a state of affairs offering the maximum freedom of choice may not be thought desirable, having regard to other social ends. To show that, in certain conditions, the maximum of freedom of this sort is achieved is not to show that those conditions should be sought after.

Moreover, there are certain limitations on the possibility of formulating ends in price offers. To secure the conditions within which the equilibrating tendencies may emerge there must exist a certain legal apparatus, not capable of being elicited by price bids, yet essential for their orderly execution.[1] The negative condition of health, immunity from infectious disease, is not an end which can be wholly achieved by individual action. In urban conditions the failure of one individual to conform to certain sanitary requirements may involve all the others in an epidemic. The securing of ends of this sort must necessarily involve the using of factors of production in a way not fully compatible with complete freedom in the expenditure of gross individual resources. And it is clear that society, acting as a body of political citizens, may formulate ends which interfere much more drastically than this with the free choices of the individuals composing it. There is nothing in the corpus of economic analysis which in itself affords any justification for regarding these ends as good or bad. Economic analysis can simply point out the implications as regards the dis-

---

[1] On the place of the legal framework of Economic Activity, the "organisation" of the Economy as he calls it, Dr. Strigl's work cited above is very illuminating. See Strigl, *op. cit.*, pp. 85-121.

posal of means of production of the various patterns of ends which may be chosen.

For this reason, the use of the adjectives "economical" and "uneconomical" to describe certain policies is apt to be very misleading. The criterion of economy which follows from our original definitions is the securing of given ends with least means. It is, therefore, perfectly intelligible to say of a certain policy that it is uneconomical, if, in order to achieve certain ends, it uses more scarce means than are necessary. As regards the disposition of means, the terms "economical" and "uneconomical" can be used with complete intelligibility.

But it is not intelligible to use them as regards ends themselves. As we have seen already, there are no economic ends.[1] There are only economical and uneconomical ways of achieving given ends. We cannot say that the pursuit of given ends is uneconomical because the ends are uneconomical; we can only say it is uneconomical if the ends are pursued with an unnecessary expenditure of means.

Thus it is not legitimate to say that going to war is uneconomical, if, having regard to all the issues and all the sacrifices necessarily involved, it is decided that the anticipated result is worth the sacrifice. It is only legitimate so to describe it if it is attempted to secure this end with an unnecessary degree of sacrifice.[2]

It is the same with measures more specifically "economic"—to use the term in its confused popular sense. If we assume that the ends of public policy are the safeguarding of conditions under which individual demands, as reflected in the price system, are satisfied

---

[1] See Chapter II., Sections 2 and 3, above.
[2] On all this see Mises, *Die Gemeinwirtschaft*, 1te Auf., pp. 112-116.

as amply as possible under given conditions, then, save
in very special circumstances which are certainly not
generally known to those who impose such measures,
it is legitimate to say that a protective tariff on
wheat is uneconomical in that it imposes obstacles
to the achievement of this end. This follows clearly
from purely neutral analysis. But if the object in view
transcends these ends—if the tariff is designed to bring
about an end not formulated in consumers' price
offers—the safeguarding of food supply against the
danger of war, for instance—it is not legitimate to say
that it is uneconomical just because it results in the
impoverishment of consumers. In such circumstances
the only justification for describing it as uneconomical
would be a demonstration that it achieved this end
also with an unnecessary sacrifice of means.[1]

Again, we may examine the case of minimum wage
regulation. It is a well-known generalisation of
Theoretical Economics that a wage which is held above
the equilibrium level necessarily involves unemployment and a diminution of the value of capital. This is
one of the most elementary deductions from the theory
of economic equilibrium. The history of this country
since the War is one long vindication of its accuracy.[2]
The popular view that the validity of these "static"
deductions is vitiated by the probability of "dynamic

[1] See a paper by the present author on *The Case of Agriculture in Tariffs:*
The Case Examined (edited by Sir William Beveridge).

[2] See Böhm-Bawerk, *Macht oder Ökonomischer Gesetz (Gesammelte
Schriften,* pp. 250-300). (This has recently been translated by Dr. J. R. Mez
of the University of Oregon under the title, *Control or Economic Law* [Eugene,
Oregon]). See also Schumpeter, *Das Grundprinzip der Verteilungstheorie
(Archiv für Sozialwissenschaft und Sozialpolitik,* vol. xlii., 1916, pp. 1-88);
W. H. Hutt, *The Theory of Collective Bargaining;* Pigou, *Unemployment,*
chs. v. and vi.; Hicks, *The Theory of Wages.* On the evidence of post-War
history, Dr. Benham's *Wages, Prices and Unemployment (Economist,* June 20,
1931) should be consulted.

improvements" induced by wage pressure, depends upon an oversight of the fact that these "improvements" are themselves one of the manifestations of capital wastage.[1] But such a policy is not *necessarily* to be described as uneconomical. If, in the society imposing such a policy, it is generally thought that the gain of the absence of wage payments below a certain rate, more than compensates for the unemployment and losses it involves, the policy cannot be described as uneconomical. As private individuals we may think that such a system of preferences sacrifices tangible increments of the ingredients of real happiness for the false end of a mere diminution of inequality. We may suspect that those who cherish such preferences are deficient in imagination. But there is nothing in scientific Economics which warrants us in passing these judgments. Economics is neutral as between ends. Economics cannot pronounce on the validity of ultimate judgments of value.

[1] It is curious that this should not have been more generally realised, for it is usually the most enthusiastic exponents of this view who also denounce most vigorously the unemployment "caused" by rationalisation. It is, of course, the necessity of the conversion of capital into forms which are profitable at the higher wage level which is responsible both for a shrinkage in social capital and the creation of an industrial structure incapable of affording full employment to the whole working population. There is no reason to expect permanent unemployment as a result of rationalisation *not* induced by wages above the equilibrium level. For this reason it is to be feared that the statistics quoted by Mr. Colin Clark in his interesting *Statistical Studies on the Present Economic Position of Great Britain* (*Economic Journal*, 1931, pp. 360-362) do not lend themselves to the interpretation he puts on them. An increase of output per head in particular industries is not necessarily an index of increased general efficiency in any sense relevant to what Mr. Clark calls "real want-satisfying power". The figure records *average* not *marginal* productivity. It takes no account of the position of the margin at which full employment is possible. It leaves completely unrevealed the question whether the capital investment which made it possible was as "productive" as alternative forms of investment profitable at other wage levels. Mr. Clark's deductions are perilously akin to the economic fallacy of misplaced concreteness discussed in Chapter III.

4. In recent years, certain economists, realising this inability of Economics, thus conceived, to provide within itself a series of principles binding upon practice, have urged that the boundaries of the subject should be extended to include normative studies. Mr. Hawtrey and Mr. J. A. Hobson, for instance, have argued that Economics should not only take account of valuations and ethical standards as given data in the manner explained above, but that also it should pronounce upon the ultimate validity of these valuations and standards. "Economics", says Mr. Hawtrey, "cannot be dissociated from Ethics".[1]

Unfortunately it does not seem logically possible to associate the two studies in any form but mere juxtaposition. Economics deals with ascertainable facts; ethics with valuations and obligations. The two fields of enquiry are not on the same plane of discourse. Between the generalisations of positive and normative studies there is a logical gulf fixed which no ingenuity can disguise and no juxtaposition in space or time bridge over. The proposition that the price of pork fluctuates with variations in supply and demand follows from a conception of the relation of pork to human impulses which, in the last resort, is verifiable by introspection and observation. We can ask people whether they are prepared to buy pork and how much they

[1] See Hawtrey, *The Economic Problem*, especially pp. 184 and 203-215, and Hobson, *Wealth and Life*, pp. 112-140. I have examined Mr. Hawtrey's contentions in some detail in an article entitled, *Mr. Hawtrey on the Scope of Economics* (*Economica*, No. 20, pp. 172-178). But in that article I made certain statements with regard to the claims of "welfare Economics" which I should now wish to formulate rather differently. Moreover, at that time I did not understand the nature of the idea of *precision* in economic generalisations, and my argument contains one entirely unnecessary concession to the critics of Economics. On the main point under discussion, however, I have nothing to retract, and in what follows I have borrowed one or two sentences from the last few paragraphs of the article.

are prepared to buy at different prices. Or we can watch how they behave when equipped with currency and exposed to the stimuli of the pig-meat markets.[1] But the proposition that it is *wrong* that pork should be valued, although it is a proposition which has greatly influenced the conduct of different races, is a proposition which we cannot conceive being verified at all in this manner. Propositions involving the verb "ought" are different in kind from propositions involving the verb "is". And it is difficult to see what possible good can be served by not keeping them separate, or failing to recognise their essential difference.[2]

All this is not to say that economists should not deliver themselves on ethical questions, any more than an argument that botany is not æsthetics is to say that botanists should not have views of their own on the lay-out of gardens. On the contrary, it is greatly to be desired that economists should have speculated long and widely on these matters, since only in this way will they be in a position to appreciate the implications as regards *given* ends of problems

---

[1] On all this it seems to me that the elucidations of Max Weber are quite definitive. Indeed, I confess that I am quite unable to understand how it can be conceived to be possible to call this part of Max Weber's methodology in question. (See *Der Sinn der "Wertfreiheit" der Soziologischen und Ökonomischen Wissenschaften, Gesammelte Aufsätze zur Wissenschaftslehre*, pp. 451-502).

[2] Mr. J. A. Hobson, commenting on a passage in my criticism of Mr. Hawtrey which was couched in somewhat similar terms, protests that "this is a refusal to recognise any empirical *modus vivendi* or contact between economic values and human values" (Hobson, *op. cit.*, p. 129). Precisely, but why should Mr. Hobson, of all men, complain? My procedure simply empties out of Economics—what Mr. Hobson himself has never ceased to proclaim to be an illegitimate intrusion—any "economic" presumption that the valuations of the market-place are ethically respectable. I cannot help feeling that a great many of Mr. Hobson's strictures on the procedure of Economic Science fall to the ground if the view of the scope of its subject-matter suggested above be explicitly adopted.

which are put to them for solution. Our methodological axioms involve no prohibition of outside interests! All that is contended is that there is no logical
connection between the two types of generalisation,
and that there is nothing to be gained by invoking the
sanctions of one to reinforce the conclusions of the
other.

And, quite apart from all questions of methodology,
there is a very practical justification for such a procedure. In the rough-and-tumble of political struggle,
differences of opinion may arise either as a result of
differences about ends or as a result of differences
about the means of attaining ends. Now, as regards
the first type of difference, neither Economics nor any
other science can provide any solvent. If we disagree
about ends it is a case of thy blood or mine—or live
and let live, according to the importance of the difference, or the relative strength of our opponents. But,
if we disagree about means, then scientific analysis
can often help us to resolve our differences. If we disagree about the morality of the taking of interest (and
we understand what we are talking about),[1] then there
is no room for argument. But if we disagree about the
objective implications of fluctuations in the rate of
interest, then economic analysis should enable us to
settle our dispute. Shut Mr. Hawtrey in a room as
Secretary of a Committee composed of Bentham,
Buddha, Lenin and the Head of the United States
Steel Corporation, set up to decide upon the ethics of
usury, and it is improbable that he could produce an
"agreed document". Set the same committee to determine the objective results of State regulation of the
rate of discount, and it ought not to be beyond human

---

[1] See below, Section 5.

ingenuity to produce unanimity—or at any rate a majority report, with Lenin perhaps dissenting. Surely, for the sake of securing what agreement we can in a world in which avoidable differences of opinion are all too common, it is worth while carefully delimiting those fields of enquiry where this kind of settlement is possible from those where it is not to be hoped for[1]—it is worth while delimiting the neutral area of science from the more disputable area of moral and political philosophy.

5. But what, then, is the significance of Economic Science? We have seen that it provides, within its own structure of generalisations, no norms which are binding in practice. It is incapable of deciding as between the desirability of different ends. It is fundamentally distinct from Ethics. Wherein, then, does its unquestionable significance consist?

Surely it consists in just this, that, when we are faced with a choice between ultimates, it enables us to choose with full awareness of the implications of what

---

[1] In fact, of course, such has been the practice of economists of the "orthodox" tradition ever since the emergence of scientific economics. See, e.g., Cantillon, *Essai sur la Nature du Commerce* (Higgs' ed., p. 85): "It is also a question outside of my subject whether it is better to have a great multitude of inhabitants poor and badly provided, than a smaller number much more at their ease". See also Ricardo, *Notes on Malthus*, p. 188: "It has been well said by M. Say that it is not the province of the Political Economist to advise—he is to tell you how you may become rich, but he is not to advise you to prefer riches to indolence or indolence to riches". Of course, occasionally among those economists who have worked with a hedonistic bias, there has been confusion of the two kinds of proposition. But this has not happened to anything like the extent commonly suggested. Most of the allegations of bias spring from unwillingness to believe the facts that economic analysis brings to light. The proposition that real wages above the equilibrium point involve unemployment is a perfectly neutral inference from one of the most elementary propositions in theoretical economics. But it is difficult to mention it in some circles without being accused, if not of sinister interest, at least of a hopeless bias against the poor and the unfortunate. Similarly at the present day it is difficult to enunciate the platitude that a general tariff on imports will affect foreign demand for our exports without being thought a traitor to one's country.

we are choosing. Faced with the problem of deciding between this and that, we are not entitled to look to Economics for the ultimate decision. There is nothing in Economics which relieves *us* of the obligation to choose. There is nothing in any kind of science which can decide the ultimate problem of preference. But, to be rational, we must know what it is we prefer. We must be aware of the objective implications of the alternatives of choice. For rationality in choice is nothing more and nothing less than choice with complete awareness of the alternatives rejected. And it is just here that Economics acquires its practical significance. It can make clear to us the implications of the different ends we may choose. It makes it possible for us to will with knowledge of what it is we are willing. It makes it possible for us to select a system of ends which are mutually consistent with each other.[1]

An example or two should make this quite clear. Let us start with a case in which the implications of one act of choice are elucidated. We may revert once more to an example we have already considered—the imposition of a protective tariff. We have seen already that there is nothing in scientific Economics which warrants our describing such a policy as good or bad. We have decided that, if such a policy is decided upon with full consciousness of the sacrifices involved, there is no justification for describing it as uneconomical. The deliberate choice by a body of citizens acting

---

[1] It is perhaps desirable to emphasise that the consistency which is made possible is a consistency of achievement, not a consistency of ends. The achievement of one end may be held to be inconsistent with the achievement of another, either on the plane of valuation, or on the plane of objective possibility. Thus it may be held to be ethically inconsistent to serve two masters at once. It is objectively inconsistent to arrange to be with each of them at the same time, at different places. It is the latter kind of inconsistency in the sphere of social policy which scientific Economics should make it possible to eliminate.

collectively to frustrate, in the interests of ends such as defence, the preservation of the countryside, and so on, their several choices as consumers, cannot be described as uneconomical or irrational, if it is done with full awareness of what is being done. But this will not be the case unless the citizens in question are fully conscious of the objective implications of the step they are taking. And in an extensive modern society it is only as a result of intricate economic analysis that they may be placed in possession of this knowledge. The great majority, even of educated people, called upon to decide upon the desirability of, let us say, protection for Agriculture, think only of the effects of such measures on the protected industry. They see that such measures are likely to benefit the industry, and hence they argue that the measures are good. But, of course, as every first year student knows, it is only here that the problem begins. To judge the further repercussions of the tariff an analytical technique is necessary. This is why in countries where the level of education in Economics is not high, there is a constant tendency to the approval of more and more protective tariffs.

Nor is the utility of such analysis to be regarded as confined to decisions on isolated measures such as the imposition of a single tariff. It enables us to judge more complicated systems of policy. It enables us to see what *sets* of ends are compatible with each other and what are not, and upon what conditions such compatibility is dependent. And, indeed, it is just here that the possession of some such technique becomes quite indispensable if policy is to be rational. It may be just possible to will rationally the achievement of particular social ends overriding individual valuations without much assistance from analysis. The case of a subsidy to protect essential food supplies is a case in point. It is almost impossible to conceive the carrying through of more elaborate policies without the aid of such an instrument.[1]

We may take an example from the sphere of monetary policy. It is an unescapable deduction from the first principles of monetary theory that, in a world in which conditions are changing at different rates in different monetary areas, it is impossible to achieve at once stable prices and stable exchanges.[2] The two ends—in this case the "ends" are quite obviously subordinate to other major norms of policy—are logically incompatible. You may try for one or you may try for the other—it is not certain that price stability is either permanently attainable or conducive to equilibrium generally—but you cannot rationally try for both. If you do, there must be a breakdown. These conclusions are well known to all economists. Yet without some analytical apparatus how few of us would perceive the incompatibility of the ends in question!

And even this is a narrow example. Without economic analysis it is not possible rationally to choose between alternative *systems* of society. We have seen

[1] All this should be a sufficient answer to those who continually lay it down that "social life is too complex a matter to be judged by economic analysis". It is because social life is so complicated that economic analysis is necessary if we are to understand even a part of it. It is usually those who talk most about the complexity of life and the insusceptibility of human behaviour to any kind of logical analysis who prove to have the most *simpliste* intellectual and emotional make-up. He who has really glimpsed the irrational in the springs of human action will have no "fear" that it can ever be killed by logic.

[2] See Keynes, *A Tract on Monetary Reform*, pp. 154-155; also an interesting paper by Mr. Dennis Robertson, *How do We Want Gold to Behave?* reprinted in the *International Gold Problem*, pp. 18-46.

already that if we regard a society which permits inequality of incomes as an evil in itself, and an equalitarian society as presenting an end to be pursued above all other things, then it is illegitimate to regard such a preference as uneconomic. But it is not possible to regard it as rational unless it is formulated with a full consciousness of the nature of the sacrifice which is thereby involved. And we cannot do this unless we understand, not only the essential nature of the capitalistic mechanism, but also the necessary conditions and limitations to which the type of society proposed as a substitute would be subject. It is not rational to will a certain end if one is not conscious of what sacrifice the achievement of that end involves. And, in this supreme weighing of alternatives, only a complete awareness of the implications of modern economic analysis can confer the capacity to judge rationally.[1]

But, if this is so, what need is there to claim any larger status for Economic Science? Is it not the burden of our time that we do not realise what we are doing? Are not our difficulties due to just this fact, that we will ends which are incompatible, not because we wish for deadlock, but because we do not realise their incompatibility. It may well be that there may exist differences as regards ultimate ends in modern society which render some conflict inevitable. But it is clear that many of our most pressing difficulties arise, not for this reason, but because our aims are not co-ordinated. As consumers we will cheapness,

---

[1] In this connection the work of Professor Mises cited above should be consulted. See also Ludwig Pohle, *Kapitalismus und Sozialismus*; Halm, *Ist der Sozialismus wirtschaftlich möglich?* and N. G. Pierson, *Das Wertproblem in der sozialistischen Gesellschaft* (*Zeitschrift für Volkswirtschaft und Sozialpolitik*, N.F., Bd. 4, pp. 607-639).

as producers we choose security. We value one distribution of factors of production as private spenders and savers. As public citizens we sanction arrangements which frustrate the achievement of this distribution. We call for cheap money and lower prices, fewer imports and a larger volume of trade.[1] The different " will-organisations " in society, although composed of the same individuals, formulate different preferences. Everywhere our difficulties seem to arise, not so much from divisions between the different members of the body politic, as from, as it were, split personalities on the part of each one of them.[2]

To such a situation, Economics brings the solvent of knowledge. It enables us to conceive the far-reaching implications of alternative possibilities of policy. It does not, and it cannot, enable us to evade the necessity of choosing between alternatives. But it does make it possible for us to bring our different choices into harmony. It cannot remove the ultimate limitations on 'human action. But it does make it possible within these limitations to act consistently. It serves for the inhabitant of the modern world with its endless interconnections and relationships as an extension of his perceptive apparatus. It provides a technique of rational action.

6. This, then, is the sense in which Economics can be truly said to assume rationality in human society. It makes no pretence, as has been alleged so often, that action is necessarily rational in the sense that the

[1] Cf. M. Ste. Braun, *Theorie der Staatlichen Wirtschaftspolitik*, p. 5.

[2] In this way economic analysis reveals still further examples of a phenomenon to which attention has often been drawn in recent discussion of the theory of Sovereignty in Public Law. See Figgis, *Churches in the Modern State*; Maitland, *Introduction to* Gierke's *Political Theories of the Middle Ages;* Laski, *The Problem of Sovereignty, Authority in the Modern State.*

ends pursued are not mutually inconsistent. There is nothing in its generalisations which necessarily implies reflective deliberation in ultimate valuation. It relies upon no assumption that individuals act rationally. But it does depend for its practical *raison d'être* upon the assumption that it is desirable that they should do so. It does assume that, within the bounds of necessity, it is desirable to choose ends which can be achieved harmoniously.

And thus in the last analysis Economics does depend, if not for its existence, at least for its significance, on an ultimate valuation—the affirmation that rationality and ability to choose with knowledge is desirable. If irrationality, if the surrender to the blind force of external stimuli and unco-ordinated impulse at every moment is a good to be preferred above all others, then it is true the *raison d'être* of Economics disappears. And it is the tragedy of our generation, red with fratricidal strife and betrayed almost beyond belief by those who should have been its intellectual leaders, that there have arisen those who would uphold this ultimate negation, this yearning for the deep unawareness of the unborn state, this escape from the tragic necessities of choice which has become conscious. With all such there can be no argument. In love with death, their love will overtake them. For them there can be no "way out" save the way which leads out of life. But for all those who still affirm more positive values, that branch of knowledge which, above all others, is the symbol and safeguard of rationality in social arrangements, must, in the anxious days which are to come, by very reason of this menace to that for which it stands, possess a peculiar and a heightened significance.

PRINTED IN GREAT BRITAIN BY
BILLING AND SONS LIMITED,
GUILDFORD AND ESHER